THE COCKTAIL BOOK

ENTERTAINING WITH DRINK AND FOOD

MICHAEL BRUNELLE

The Cocktail Book, Entertaining
with Drink and Food

Printed by Caxton Printers, Caldwell, Idaho.

Eighth edition revised and updated.

first printing 1984
second printing 1985
third printing 1987
fourth printing 1989
fifth printing 1991
sixth printing 1994
seventh printing 1998

Library of Congress Catalog Card Number: 98-71417
ISBN 0-9664834-0-5

Published by Beatriz Cortabarria
1327 Pin Oak Court
Charlottesville, VA 22901

The eighth revised version of *The Cocktail Book* boasts several new and popular recipes while maintaining the successful text and design of the previous edition. I always like to point out that this tome has come a long way from its humble yet honest beginnings as the little black book that I carried to many restaurants and cocktail lounges to note the variations and new recipes that were unique to those places.

This incarnation of those labored scratchings has been arranged into three parts:

The first begins with **Glassware** and continues through **Food**, covering the tools, skills and recipes that are needed to properly serve customers or guests. The section on **Wine** has helpful information for people who enjoy dining out, and the **Parties** and **Food** sections will be of interest to those hosting a gathering of any size.

The second part consists of drink recipes, **Cocktails, Martinis, Mocktails** and some **Popular New Recipes**, designed with the busy bartender in mind. All are listed in alphabetical order so they can be quickly located, and they are clear and easy to read. Among them are the 100 most popular drinks in America, as well as over one hundred additional interesting and tasty mixtures. The ingredients, all common and widely available, are listed in the order that they are to be mixed.

The third part offers further information related to the recipes. The **Index** lists all of the drinks by ingredient. This will be helpful if you do not know the name of a certain cocktail, or if you wish to see what can be mixed using a particular liquor or liqueur. The **Ingredients** section explains what the different liqueurs are, and the **Definitions** pages will clue you in on some of the language you may hear when sitting at the bar.

I hope you will find this book useful and interesting whether entertaining, working in a bar or restaurant, or studying up for a night on the town.

Michael Brunelle

GLASSWARE

Three types of glassware are in general use in hotels and restaurants today. The familiar, flat based glasses are used for highballs. Those with a decorative footed base keep tabletops from getting wet, since condensation does not form on the base. Stemware is used for drinks that are served cold but without ice. The stem allows the glass to be held without warming the contents with one's hand.

Highball glasses are used for liquors mixed with water, soda or soft drinks.

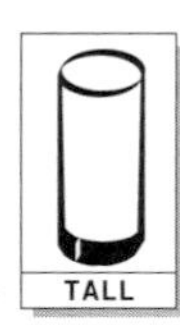

Tall highball glasses are used for any liquor mixed with fruit juice or tonic water, for any cordial with club soda, the Cuba Libre and any highball requested in a tall glass.

The sour glass is used for sours, although many bars use a larger glass that can also be used for other types of cocktails.

Snifters are designed to be held in the palm of the hand, which will warm it and direct delicious brandy fumes into the nose. They are often used for other premium liqueurs as well.

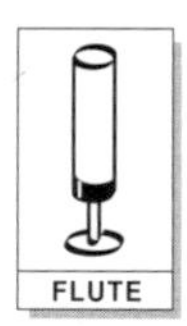

Flute and **tulip** shaped glasses work best for champagne, since they are attractive and preserve the bubbles longer than a saucer will.

Shot glasses are used for all liquors served straight or "neat".

Martini glasses are used for all martinis and variations served "up".

The popular tulip shaped **sherry glass** is actually a bit small for the standard two ounce serving. But the traditional sherry glass is rarely seen in establishments in the United States.

The 6 ounce **all purpose wine glass** is very popular, and used for many cocktails and coffee drinks as well as red, white and rosé wines. The pros put a spoon in the glass before adding hot coffee to prevent cracking in glasses that haven't been heat treated.

Old fashioned glasses are also known as **"rocks glasses"**, and are used for a variety of short drinks, including straight liquor served "on the rocks".

Large cocktail glasses are used for frozen drinks.

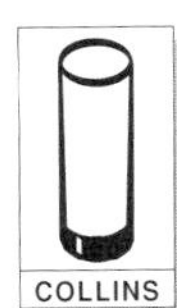

Collins glasses are used for Slings, Collins and other long drinks.

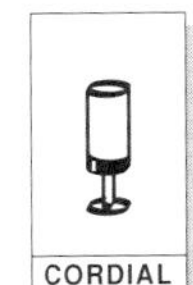

Cordial glasses are used for liqueurs and pousse cafes.

Coffee mugs are used for all hot drinks. Preheat them by filling them with hot water (and then dumping it) so they won't draw heat from the drink.

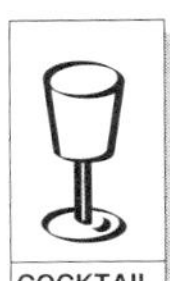

Cocktail glasses are used for mixed drinks that are shaken or blended and strained.

UTENSILS

Certain utensils are indispensable in the bar. Most of them can be found in your kitchen, but some are specialized tools, and you may have to go to a restaurant supply store to find them.

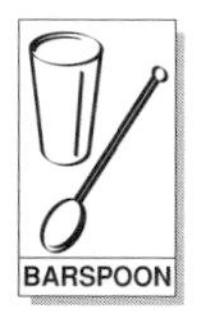

A long handled bar spoon for stirring and for floating liqueurs.

A stirring glass and **wire strainer** for stirred cocktails. Stirring is employed when wines and clear liquors are mixed. The clear drinks, mainly martinis, are just as good when shaken and perhaps even colder, but shaking produces a cloudy looking cocktail.

A cocktail shaker is used when cream, eggs, sugar or juices were among the ingredients. They are becoming popular again, but most bartenders still use electric blenders.

A blender with two mixing cans, one with sharp blades for making slushy drinks, and one with blunt blades for cocktails that are to be shaken and strained.

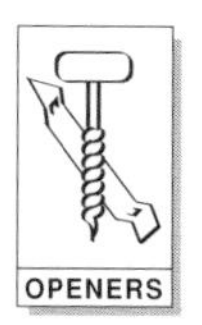

A can opener, a bottle opener and **a good corkscrew** for getting into cans and bottles.

A knife and **cutting board** for making garnish.

JIGGER

The measuring cup or **jigger** can vary in size from 1/2 to 1-1/2 ounces. The 1 ounce size is known as a pony, the 1-1/2 as a jigger. Most bars pour a 1-1/4 ounce drink, and many barmen pour by eye or else have an automatic liquor dispenser. A jigger should be used until you learn to pour by feel.

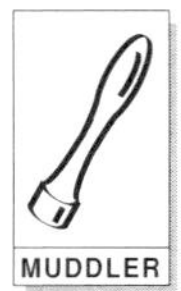
MUDDLER

The muddler or **muddle stick** is used to crush together sugar cubes, bitters and fruit when making Old Fashioneds and Sazeracs. It can also be used to make crushed ice by wrapping ice cubes in a bar towel and beating them into small pieces.

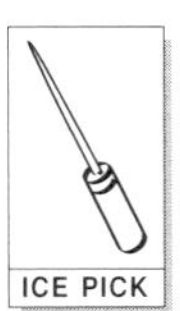
ICE PICK

An ice pick for breaking up chunks of ice and also peeling lemons (see garnish pages).

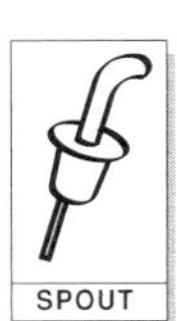
SPOUT

Pour spouts are commonly used in cocktail lounges. They keep the bartender from spilling liquor all over the place, and they make it easier to measure by eye. Professional bar people can be quite accurate using spouts and the "three count" pour. It takes a lot of practice to develop a feel for measuring this way, and many bars require their employees to use a jigger for measuring. The straighter of the two spouts (#2) is for use with juices and mix, while the curved model is slower and is used for liquor.

SPOUT #2

ixed drinks are concocted in various ways, depending on the ingredients and the preferences of the person for whom the drink is made.

Highballs, fruit juice drinks and many drinks served "on the rocks" are **built**, that is, mixed right in the glass in which they will be served.

Drinks made of two or more spirits, or spirits and wine, are **stirred** to mix and cool them without diluting them too much. They are then strained into a stemmed glass.

A drink is **shaken** when cream, eggs, sugar and sometimes juices are ingredients. Most bartenders use electric blenders, but there are still some traditionalists out there.

Any drink that is shaken can be **blended**, but I don't think they are as good as a shaken cocktail. Frozen drinks, or any using fresh fruit or ice cream, must be blended. There are blender cans with blunt blades for drinks that would be shaken, and sharp blades for drinks made with ice or solid food.

STIR AND STRAIN

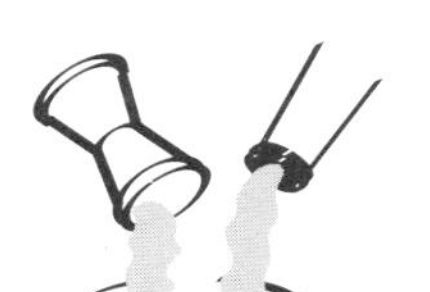

Stir briskly, 8 or 10 turns to chill but not dilute cocktail.

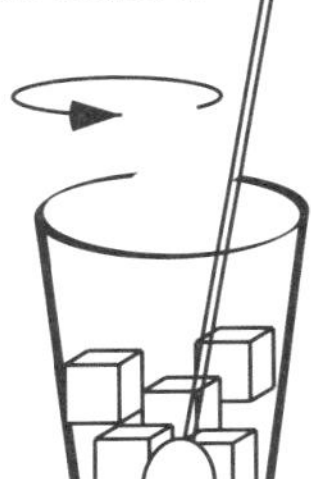

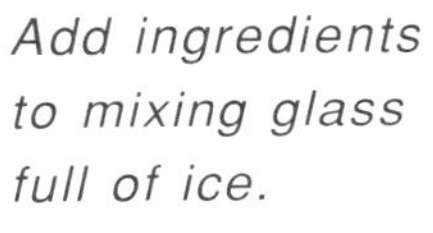

Add ingredients to mixing glass full of ice.

Strain into chilled glasses, fill all half-way and then even them out.

BLEND AND STRAIN

Combine ice and ingredients in blender can.

Mix for a few seconds and immediately strain into cocktail glasses and serve.

FLAMING DRINKS

Some drinks are **flamed**, which means that a small amount of spirit, often a 151 proof rum, is floated on top of the cocktail mixture and lit on fire. This is done for presentation purposes only, and does not affect the taste of the drink at all. Be sure the flame is put out before anyone tries to take a sip of the drink.

FLOATING CREAM + LIQUEURS

Many coffee drinks call for whipped cream as the final touch. If the whipped cream you are using is thick but not stiff enough to hold any shape, it must be carefully **floated.**

Pousse cafe style cocktails are back in fashion now, and they also require careful construction to achieve a pretty layered effect.

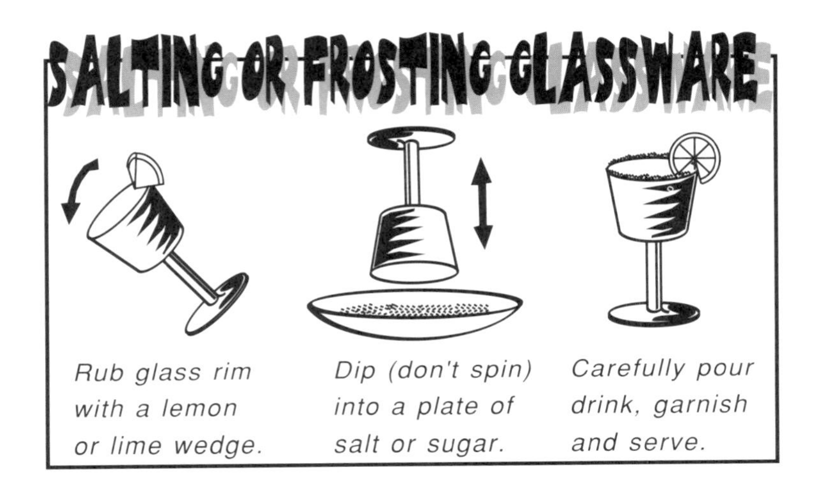

Frosting a glass has two meanings. It is either to chill a glass by putting it in a freezer or crushed ice so that it will frost when taken out to be used, (common practice for beer mugs and martini glasses), or to put sugar on the rim of a glass, in the same manner that salt is put on for a Margarita.

Heating a snifter before pouring brandy or a liqueur into it will increase the aroma and enhance the flavor. The snifter was designed to direct the fumes to the nose of the drinker. Half the pleasure of a good brandy is inhaling the wonderful vapors. To heat the glass, fill it with very hot water and let it stand for a couple of minutes. Empty the glass, pour the liqueur and serve immediately.

GARNISH

The fruit or vegetable garnish is a very important part of a cocktail. It is the final touch that dresses the drink with a little color, and it also adds a bit of flavor. Be sure to use unblemished fruit and rinse it well before cutting. And be sure not to cut more than you need, because garnish is always better when it is fresh.

These are the most commonly used garnish:

Wedges (squeezes) cut from lemons or limes.

Slices (wheels) cut from lemons or limes.

Half slices usually cut from oranges.

Strips (twists) of lemons and sometimes oranges.

Sticks of celery, sometimes referred to as "trees".

Pearl cocktail onions for Gibson martinis.

Maraschino cherries used alone or combined with other fruit to make an attractive garnish such as the "flag", where they are attached to a quarter slice of orange with a toothpick.

Green olives, pitted and stuffed with pimento. On rare occasions olives stuffed with an almond or anchovies may be used.

CUTTING LEMON TWISTS

Cut off ends of lemon.

Make a slit around each end separating yellow peel from white pith.

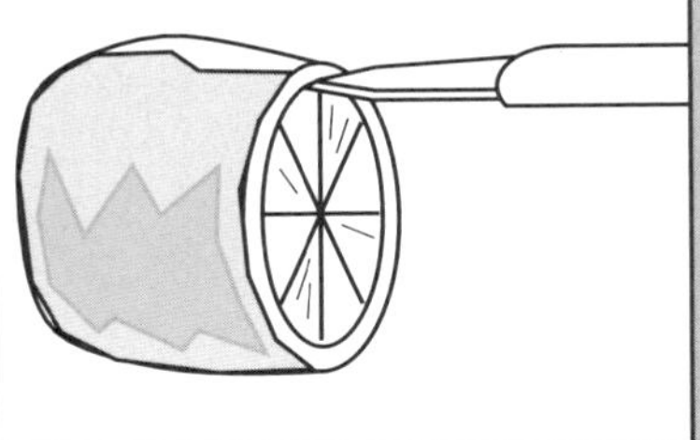

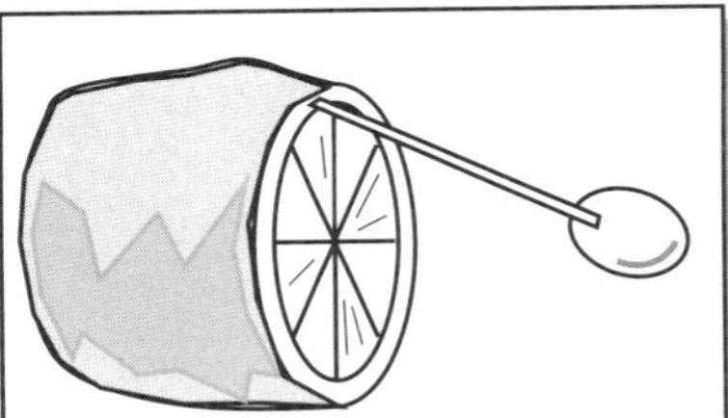

Run end of barspoon around to separate peel to halfway point, repeat from other side.

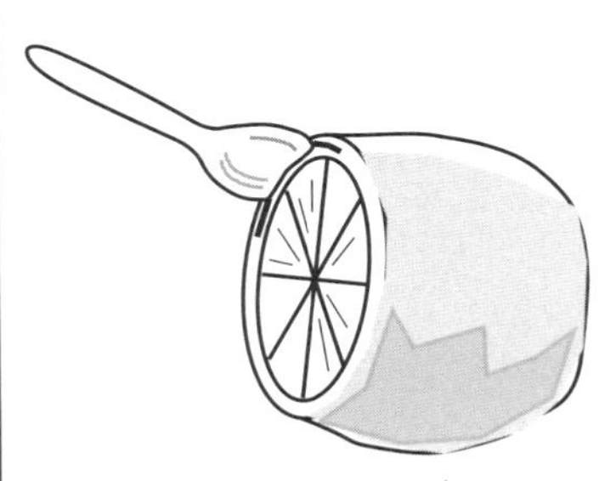

Or you can use the bowl of a soup spoon.

Slice peel open to remove from lemon.

Peel can now be sliced into twists.

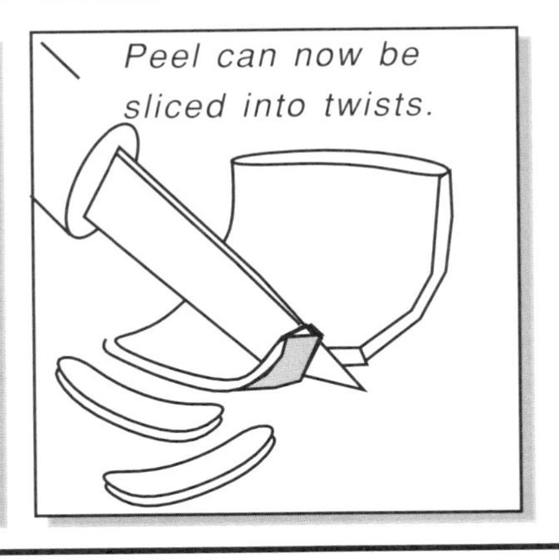

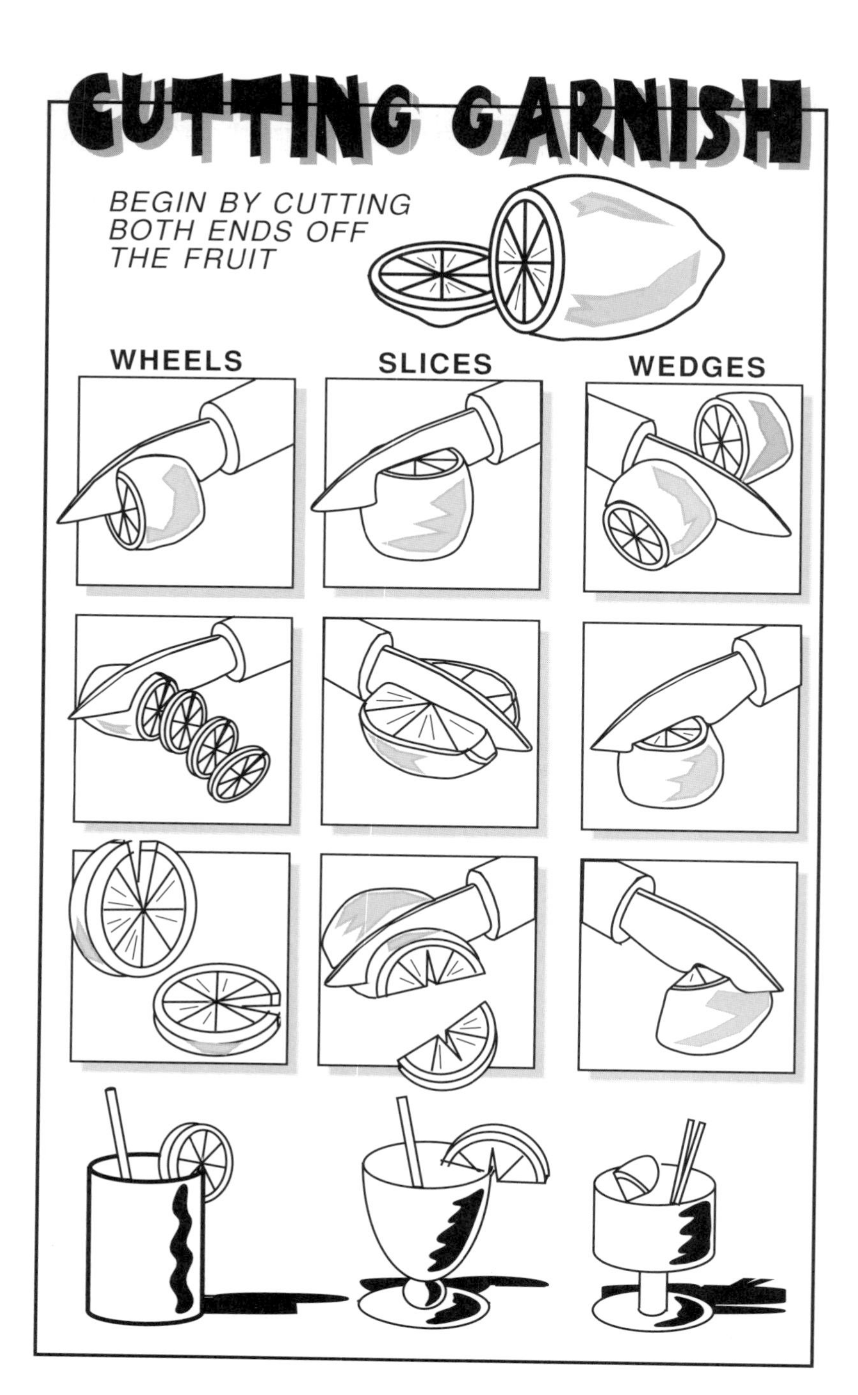
CUTTING GARNISH
BEGIN BY CUTTING BOTH ENDS OFF THE FRUIT
WHEELS
SLICES
WEDGES

Cocktail onions are used in the Gibson Cocktail.
Fruit slices sit on edge of glass.
A flag is made with a cherry and an orange wedge.
Rub glass rim with lemon twist
Drop a cherry right into a Sour.
Squeeze lime wedges then drop them in.
A celery stick, with or without the leaves left on, garnishes a Bloody Mary.
The classic Martini olive is green and stuffed with a red pimento.
Wheels slide over edge of glass.

WINE

Wine is made in many varieties and styles around the world, and is enjoyed in different ways. In America we drink it by the glass, mix it in cocktails, or even use it as an ingredient in foods and sauces. There are so many wines in the world today that it is impossible for a person to even be aware of them, much less taste them all. Wine writers do their best to describe and rate the world's wines for us. But the only way to really learn about wine is to drink wine.

What is seemingly a large body of rules governing the use of wine are actually customs and traditions that are the result of generations of experience. To these guidelines you must add your own experiences and personal preferences, keeping in mind the one firm rule that must not be forgotten: wine is to be enjoyed.

The following comments are offered with the hope that they will help you enjoy serving and drinking wine, whether during the cocktail hour or at a formal dinner.

In general, red wines are full bodied and dry, and they go well with red meat and hearty sauces. There are some white wines that will stand up to such fare, like a Sauvignon Blanc, but it is safer to stick to the reds until you have experimented a bit.

White wines run the gamut from sugary to bone dry; the medium-sweet to dry wines are good with fish and fowl dishes. The sweetest wines are better with dessert.

Rosés and blush wines tend to be on the sweet side. They are often chosen as a compromise between red and white, but will work with any dish that goes well with a white wine.

Both whites and rosés are popular as an aperitif, and they are used more often than reds in wine cocktails.

Since red wine is fuller-bodied, it is served at room temperature or slightly below. White and rosé wines are cooled to about 45 or 50 degrees. They are more volatile, at room temperature the alcohol begins to vaporize, and will

OPENING WINE

Cut foil below bulge to remove. Wipe off top of cork.

Insert screw just off center and twist all the way in.

With lever on rim of bottle, lift slowly.

When nearly out of bottle, cork can be carefully helped along.

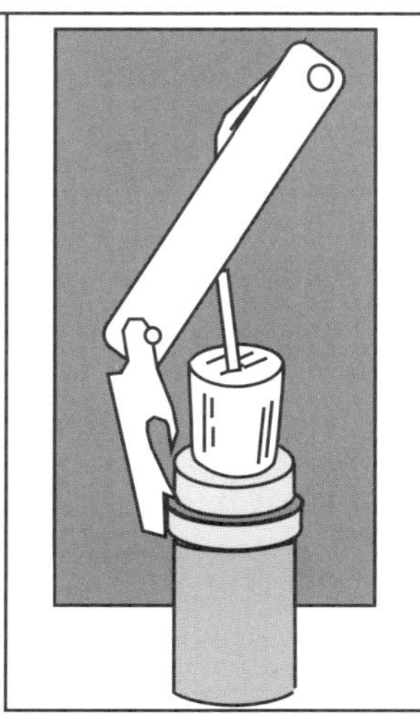

overpower the wine's fragrance. An hour in the refrigerator or fifteen to twenty minutes on ice should be enough to cool these properly.

The joy of wine is threefold; its color pleases the eye and adds beauty to the table, its fragrance pleases the nose and enhances the third aspect, its taste. The proper glass can make wine more enjoyable. A clear glass shows off color better than a tinted one; it should be large enough to fill 1/3 to 1/2 full and still hold a gracious serving, allowing one to swirl the liquid around to help release the aroma which will be directed to the nose by the shape of the glass. Open red wines ahead of time and let them breathe for an hour to improve their bouquet.

Some restaurants make a bit of a fuss when it comes to wine. But there are reasons for the great show made of serving it. This is the way it is often done: first, the waiter will show you the bottle and tell you what wine it is. This is to make sure that it is the bottle that you ordered, for once a bottle has been opened it cannot be recorked and certainly not resold. When the bottle is opened the person who ordered it will be presented with the cork. Supposedly the cork is to be smelled and examined for clues as to whether the wine has gone bad because of the cork drying out or being rotten, in either case letting air into the bottle. A wine writer once pointed out that it makes more sense to smell the wine itself; anyway, you will know how the wine is when you taste it. The host is served a small amount to taste, and if he deems the wine acceptable the rest of the guests will be served. It is rare to be served a bottle that has gone bad, and most of the bottles sent back are rejected by people trying to impress others with their knowledge. Most good restaurants will exchange a bottle that is pronounced bad.

If you are serving guests at home you can dispense with much of the show. But a good host will serve himself first so that any cork crumbs or floating matter will end up in his own glass and not a guest's.

OPENING CHAMPAGNE

When opening, point bottle in a safe direction.

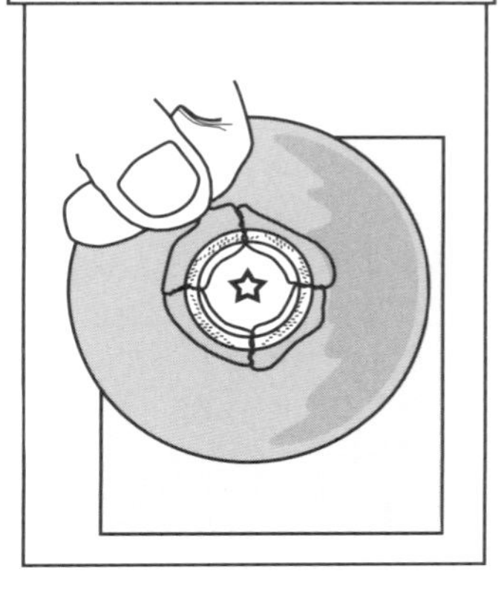

Remove foil. Unwind twisted wire and take off metal cap.

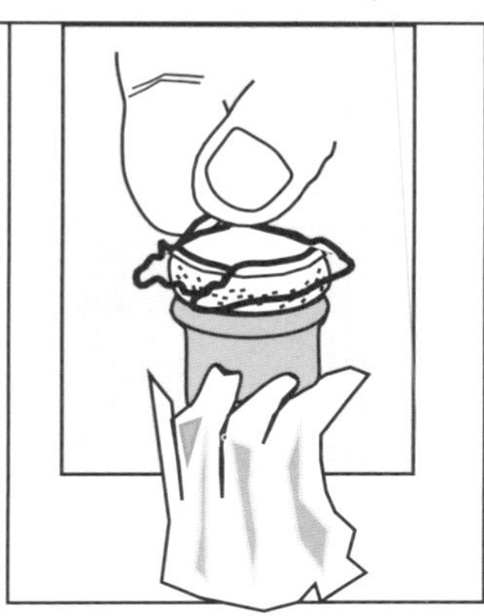

Grasp cork with towel and turn bottle to slowly work it out.

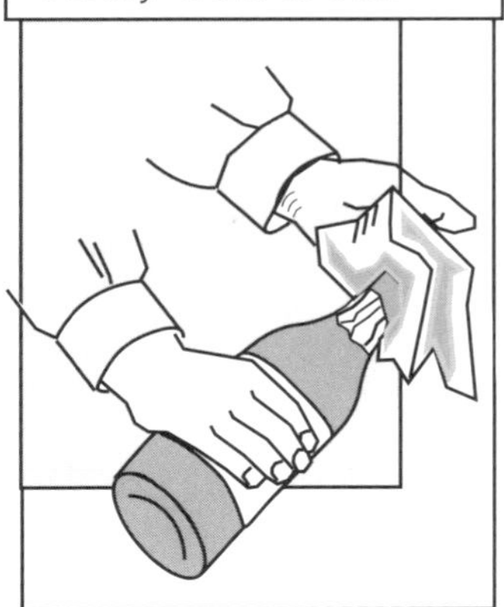

Foaming can be reduced by tipping bottle to increase surface area of champagne.

PARTIES

When planning a party at home, a few details have to be taken into account before setting up your bar. Careful preparation is the secret to being a genial and relaxed host or hostess.

Is it to be a cocktail party or a dinner party? More wine will be used at a dinner party, and usually the more food served, the more wine consumed. The cocktail party emphasizes socializing and conversation, but remember that some kind of food should always be served with alcohol.

What season is it? Light colored spirits like gin and vodka are summer favorites but whiskey and brandy become more popular as the weather gets colder. Wine is also more popular during the summer. Each season has its traditional drinks that you will want to keep in mind for your party. For example, the Tom and Jerry and Egg Nog during the winter, tonics and coolers in the summer.

The time of day can also make a difference. Bloody Marys and Screwdrivers are sometimes considered morning drinks because they are made with juices. Champagne has become very popular with brunches. Highballs and wine are most appetizing later in the day, and brandy and the whiskeys are good after dinner, as are cordials.

Another factor is the age of your guests. Older people favor dark liquors and martinis, while younger ones like the light liquors and wine and beer. Please keep in mind, these are only guidelines to help decide what to lay in, not hard and fast rules.

The bar can be set on a table or two, away from traffic areas, since people tend to congregate around the bar. If there will be fewer than 15 guests, it can be a self-service

TIPS ON KEEPING THE LIFE OF YOUR PARTY ALIVE

PLANNING THE PARTY

1. Always serve food with alcohol.
2. Have several jiggers at the bar, so mixed drinks can be measured.
3. If you serve an alcoholic punch, make it with a non-carbonated base.
4. Have non-alcoholic beverages available for your guests.
5. Don't force drinks on your guests.
6. Stop serving alcohol about an hour before the party is to end.

AFTER THE PARTY

1. Make the suggestion to your guests that you drive them home.
2. Suggest that your guest stays overnight at your home.
3. If your guest insists on driving, try to take the car keys away.
4. Call a taxi and have your guest taken home.

affair or the host can do the mixing. It might be a good idea to get a bartender for larger parties. One with a little experience should be able to handle up to 100 people. Keep the bar simple. Olives, lemon twists, lime wedges and maybe some cherries are all the garnish that you'll need. Don't bother with a blender, without running water and a dump sink at hand you'll only be creating messes and headaches. Most caterers don't even bother to take mixing glasses, and they get away with it because nowadays the majority of martini drinkers enjoy their martinis on the rocks.

Here is a list of what to lay in for a basic bar. Gin and vodka are the most popular light liquors, especially in summer. You can also buy a bottle of tequila if you are planning for a young crowd, or if you want to serve Margaritas as part of a Mexican dinner. (If you are going to get involved with blended specialty drinks I would suggest limiting yourself to one kind and perhaps beer and wine).

Bourbon, scotch and maybe a blended whiskey will take care of the dark liquors, and brandy can be included if you know that one of your guests prefers it.

A bottle each of dry vermouth and sweet vermouth for Martinis and Manhattans. Little of these are used, though they are necessary ingredients, so buy small bottles if they are available.

If you are having a dinner party, you may want to offer your guests an after dinner liqueur. This can get pretty expensive and complicated, so it is best to have just one kind, or even offer a choice between a liqueur and a brandy.

Light beer is now as popular as regular beer. Any good brand will do. Beer drinkers are fiercely loyal to their brand when talking about beer, but I've never seen one turn a brew down just because "his" beer wasn't available.

White wine is by far the favorite when taken as an aperitif. If wine is to be served with a buffet or dinner you will want to take into account what kind of food is being served. Speaking of brands, don't go overboard when buying for your bar. Inexpensive wines are fine for cocktails, and they are used for wine cocktails in the best bars. You may pick up a name brand whiskey or scotch if you know there will be a particular guest that likes it, but keep it simple and don't load up the bar with all the big names. Nobody will really notice the difference if the company and conversation are right and all are having fun.

The Cocktail Party. Allow two cocktails, glasses of wine or beer per person during the first hour of the party. One and one half servings per person each additional hour.

The Dinner Party. Allow one half bottle (two servings) of wine or champagne per person at dinner. If the dinner will last longer than usual due to extra courses or good conversation, plan on about a bottle per person.

COCKTAIL PARTY				DINNER
	servings			Bottles of wine
GUESTS	2 Hrs.	3 Hrs.	4 Hrs.	
4	8	14	20	2 or 3
5	10	18	25	3
6	12	21	30	3 or 4
7	14	25	35	4
8	16	28	40	4 or 5
9	18	32	45	5
10	20	35	50	5 or 6

CHEESE AND APPLE

Cut small squares of a cheese of your choice (the hard and aged kinds work best).
Peel an apple and cut it into small squares.
Combine the two ingredients with a party toothpick and serve them cool.

DATES WITH CREAM CHEESE AND ALMONDS

Fresh dates
Cream cheese
Milk
Ground almonds
Toasted, chopped almonds

Split the dates lengthwise along the top and remove the pit. Soften the cream cheese with a little milk and stir in a small amount of ground almonds. Place the mixture in a pastry bag and fill the dates. Then dip the top of the cream cheese into the toasted almonds so that it becomes coated in nuts.

GREEN ONION DIP

1 cup	mayonnaise
1 cup	sour cream
1/2 cup	sliced green onions
1/2 cup	parsley
1 tsp	Dijon mustard
1 clove	garlic, crushed

Mix all ingredients until smooth. Cover and chill.

HAM AND MELON ROLLUPS

Cut a ripe honeydew melon into bite size squares. Roll thinly cut prosciutto style ham, and place it over the melon on a party toothpick. Serve cool.

HOT SAUCE

28 oz can	crushed tomatoes
1 clove	garlic, crushed
1/4 - 1/2	onion, chopped
1 tsp	sugar
5	jalapeño peppers, chopped
2 tsp	vinegar
2-3 tsp	cooking oil
Salt to taste	

Mix all ingredients well.

OLIVE PUFFS

1 1/3 cups	flour
1/4 tsp	pepper
1/2 cup	grated cheddar cheese
2	egg yolks, beaten
3/4 cups	beer

Pimento stuffed olives (as many as desired)
Oil for frying, enough to cover the olives.

Mix first 4 ingredients. Stir in beer gradually.
Arrange olives on toothpicks and dip them in the batter.
Meanwhile heat oil in a skillet, until hot. Drop the coated olives into the skillet and fry them until golden.

RAITA

1 package	unsalted peanuts
1 clove	garlic, crushed
1 small bunch	coriander
3 - 4	cucumbers, grated
plain yogurt	to taste

In a blender, blend peanuts, garlic, coriander and a small amount of yogurt (enough to make the blades work).
Pour mixture over cucumbers, add yogurt to desired consistency, and mix.
Serve it with pita bread cut into triangles.

FOOD

ROQUEFORT AND CELERY

Cut celery into 2 inch lengths.
Mix to taste: Roquefort cheese
Finely chopped onion
Butter
Paprika

Spread mixture over the celery and serve it cold.

SOUR CREAM AND OLIVE DIP

1 pint	sour cream
1 clove	garlic
1 1/2 cups	chopped olives
1 tsp	Worcestershire sauce
1/2 tsp	paprika
1 tsp	onion, grated
1 tsp	lemon juice

Pepper to taste

Mix all ingredients
Serve it as a dip for vegetables.

STUFFED CHILES

Green chile peppers (as many as desired)
3 cups of cheddar (or Monterey Jack) cheese

Cut stems off of peppers and pull seeds out. Steam peppers in a steamer for a few minutes, until fairly soft. Stuff them with cheese and place them on a baking sheet. Bake them in a 350º oven until the cheese melts. You may sprinkle cheese over the top a few minutes before they are cooked completely.

You may serve this dish with hot sauce and beer.

STUFFED SNOW PEAS

Fresh snow peas
Boursin cheese
Milk

Top and tail the snow peas and plunge them into boiling salted water for 3 minutes, then immediately into cold water. Drain and pat dry. With a very sharp knife, split the snow peas on the curved side. Soften the cheese with a little milk and place in a large pastry bag with a medium plain tip. Pipe cheese into each snow pea.

TOMATO AND FRESH BASIL SALAD

Several ripe firm tomatoes
Mozzarella cheese
Fresh basil leaves

Cut the tomato and the mozzarella into slices. Place them on a platter, first the tomato slice followed by the mozzarella slice on top. Top off each grouping with a basil leaf.

Sprinkle olive oil to taste over the salad. Season with salt.

THREE CHEESE SPREAD

8 oz	bleu cheese
8 oz	cheddar cheese, finely grated
8 oz	cream cheese
3 tbs	onion, grated
1 1/2 tsp	Worcestershire sauce

Soften and mix cheeses. Add other ingredients and mix until smooth. Serve cold with bread or crackers.

BLOODY MARY MIX

(Makes 1 gallon)

3 tbs	salt or celery salt
1 tbs	pepper
6 tbs	Worcestershire sauce
1 tbs	Tabasco sauce
1 tbs	beef broth
2- 46 oz cans	tomato juice

BOB RENNER'S CHAMPAGNE PUNCH

(Makes about 1 gallon)

2 bottles	champagne
2 quarts	ginger ale
2 oz	brandy
2 oz	maraschino liqueur (optional)
4 oz	Rose's lime juice
Lemon slices	

If you decide to mix up a punch of your own, do not use only citrus (acidic) juices. According to Bob Renner, a bottle of Mai Tai mix will really add some flavor to a punch, whether it has alcohol or not. He also liked to use grenadine for both color and sweetening.

HOT BUTTERED RUM BATTER

The original hot buttered rum was nothing more than rum in sweetened hot water and a pat of butter floating on top. The modern version can be made by stirring together equal measures of brown sugar and butter, adding ground clove and cinnamon to taste.

HOT SPICED CIDER (MULLED CIDER)

Follow the recipe for Hot Spiced Wine substituting apple cider for the red wine.

HOT SPICED WINE (MULLED WINE)

One bottle	red wine (750 ml)
5 -10	cloves
Two dashes	Angostura bitters
4 tsp	sugar
2 pinches	allspice
Ground cinnamon	

Combine and heat in a heavy saucepan. Do not allow to boil. Strain. Serve in mugs with a cinnamon stick and/or slices of fruit.

SANGRIA

1 bottle	red wine (dry)
Sugar	to taste
1 bottle	club soda
A dash	brandy
A little cinnamon (optional)	
Sliced fruit (oranges, lemons, apples)	

Combine all but the soda and mix well. Refrigerate and add club soda at serving time.

SUGAR SYRUP

Many use this instead of sugar, as it mixes more easily with cold liquids.

Combine 3 cups of sugar with 1 cup of cold water. Boil for a few minutes, then cool and bottle. This will keep for years.

WHIPPED CREAM

I recommend half whipped cream for bar use, as it makes coffee drinks look more elegant, and more enjoyable to sip.

1 quart whipped cream
8 tsp sugar
1/2 oz Amaretto or any liquor (optional)

Whip until thick, but don't let it get stiff.

ALABAMA SLAMMER

Build

1/2 oz Amaretto
1/2 oz Southern Comfort
1/2 oz sloe gin

Splash of bar sour

ALEXANDER

Blend or shake and strain

3/4 oz gin
3/4 oz dark creme de cacao
3/4 oz half and half

Surprisingly good.

ALMOND JOY (TOASTED ALMOND)

Float or serve on the rocks

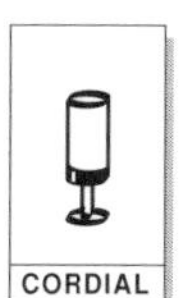

3/4 oz Kahlua
3/4 oz Amaretto
3/4 oz half and half

Sometimes you feel like a nut.

AMERICANO

Build

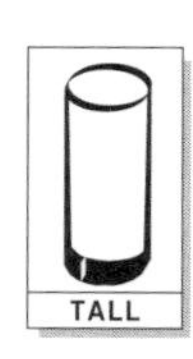

1 1/4 oz Campari
1 1/4 oz sweet vermouth

Fill with club soda

Garnish with a lemon twist

You may prefer this with a little less vermouth.

HERE'S A TOAST TO ALL WHO ARE HERE,

ANGEL'S TIP

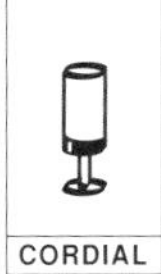

Float in order

1 oz	dark creme de cacao
1/2 oz	half and half

When served on the rocks, this is called a King Alphonse.

ANGEL'S WING

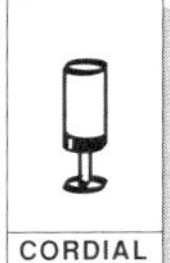

Float in order

1/2 oz	brandy
1/2 oz	white creme de cacao
1/2 oz	half and half

Garnish with a feather.

B 51

Float in order

1/2 oz	Kahlua
1/2 oz	Bailey's Irish Cream
1/2 oz	Amaretto

B 52 (NUTCRACKER)

Float in order

1/2 oz	Kahlua
1/2 oz	Bailey's Irish Cream
1/2 oz	Gran Marnier

B 53

Float in order

1/2 oz	Kahlua
1/2 oz	Bailey's Irish Cream
1/2 oz	Absolute vodka

BACARDI COCKTAIL

Blend and strain

1 1/4 oz	Bacardi rum
1/2 oz	grenadine
2 oz	sweetened lime juice

BAHAMA MAMA

Build

1 1/4 oz rum

Fill with ginger ale
Splash with sweetened lime juice

BANANA DAIQUIRI

Blend and freeze

1 oz	light rum
1/2 oz	creme de banana
3 oz	bar sour
1/2	fresh banana (optional)

Go for the banana!

BANSHEE

Blend and strain

3/4 oz	creme de banana
3/4 oz	light creme de cacao
3/4 oz	half and half
1/2	fresh banana (optional)

What do a banana and a banshee have in common? Don't ask me!

BAY BREEZE

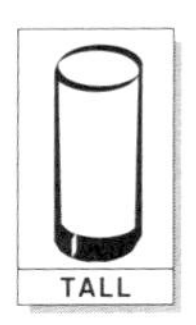

Build

1 1/4 oz	vodka
3 oz	pineapple juice
1 oz	cranberry juice

This is breakfast in San Francisco.

BELLINI

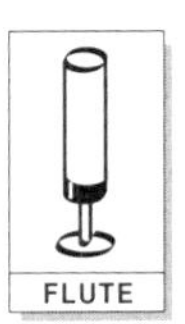

In a champagne glass

2 tbs	peach puree
1 tsp	sugar

Fill with champagne

You can substitute 1 oz peach brandy for the puree and sugar.

BENEDICTINE AND BRANDY (B & B)

3/4 oz	Benedictine Liqueur
3/4 oz	brandy

This mixture is available bottled from the makers of Benedictine.

BETWEEN THE SHEETS

Blend and strain

3/4 oz rum
3/4 oz brandy
3/4 0z triple sec
1 1/2 oz bar sour

BLACK RUSSIAN

Build

1 1/2 oz vodka
3/4 oz Kahlua

BLOODY BULL (BLOODY MARIA)

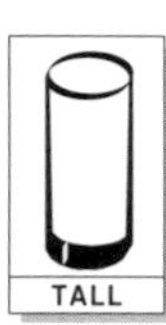

Build

1 1/4 oz tequila
2 dashes Worcestershire sauce
1 dash Tabasco sauce
celery salt
black pepper

Try a jalapeño pepper for garnish.

Fill with tomato juice

Garnish with celery and lime wedge

BLOODY MARY

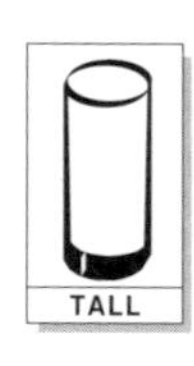

Build

1 1/4 oz vodka
2 dashes Worcestershire sauce
1 dash Tabasco sauce
celery salt
black pepper

You can salt the rim of the glass with regular or celery salt.

Fill with tomato juice

Garnish with celery and lime wedge

BLUE HAWAIIAN

Blend and strain over ice

1 oz light rum
3/4 oz blue curaçao
1 splash coconut syrup

Fill with pineapple juice

This is basically a piña colada made with blue curaçao.

BLUEBERRY TEA

In a warmed mug

3/4 oz Amaretto
3/4 oz Gran Marnier

Fill with hot tea

This is also good as iced tea

BOCCIE BALL

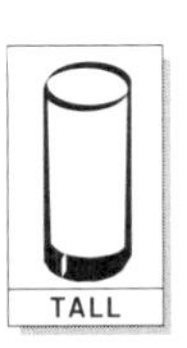

Build

1 1/4 oz Amaretto

Fill with orange juice
Splash of soda

BOILERMAKER

1 1/4 oz bourbon

Glass of beer

Serve whiskey neat with beer as a chaser

Some people pour the shot into the beer and then drink it fast.

BRANDY ALEXANDER

Blend and strain

3/4 oz brandy
3/4 oz dark creme de cacao
3/4 oz half and half

Sprinkle with nutmeg

BRAVE BULL

Build

1 1/2 oz tequila
3/4 oz Kahlua

BRUNELLE

Blend and strain

1 oz Pernod
3 oz lemon juice
1 1/2 tsp sugar

No, I did not invent this one. It goes back at least as far as the 1930's.

BUBBLE GUM SHOOTER

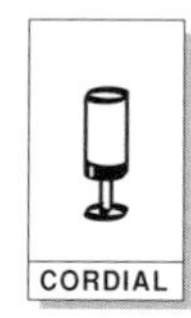

Build

3/4 oz Midori
3/4 oz Amaretto

Splash of half and half

Garnish with a cherry

BULLSHOT

Build

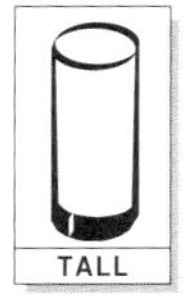
TALL

1 1/4 oz vodka
1 dash Tabasco sauce
celery salt
black pepper

Fill with: 1/2 tomato juice
1/2 beef bouillon

Garnish with celery and lime wedge

You can use bouillon straight from the can, or mix up some powdered or cubed bouillon beforehand.

BURNT ALMOND

Float or on the rocks

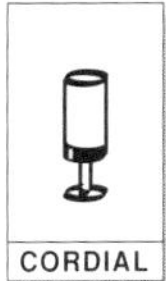
CORDIAL

1/2 oz Kahlua
1/2 oz Tia Maria
1/2 oz Amaretto

It doesn't really taste burnt.

BURRAS PEG

Build in a large snifter

SNIFTER

Champagne

1/2 oz Cognac
1/2 oz Cointreau

No need to use expensive champagne for this one.

CAFE FRANGELICO

In a warmed mug

COFFEE

3/4 oz Frangelico
3/4 oz brandy

Fill with coffee
Top with whipped cream

CAFE INTERNATIONAL

In a warmed mug

3/4 oz Amaretto
3/4oz Kahlua

Fill with coffee
Top with whipped cream

CAFE ROYAL

In a warmed mug

1/2 oz brandy or bourbon

Fill with coffee
Sugar to taste

This is traditionally served without whipped cream.

CALYPSO COFFEE

In a warmed mug

3/4 oz rum
3/4 oz Kahlua

Fill with coffee
Top with whipped cream

Tastes better with dark rum.

CALYPSO NIGHTFALL

Blend and strain

3/4 oz Kahlua
3/4 oz Amaretto
1/4 oz Galliano
1 oz half and half

Garnish with shaved chocolate

CAMPARI AND SODA

Build

1 1/4 oz Campari

Fill with soda

CANDY APPLE

Build

1 1/4 oz peppermint schnapps
1/2 oz cherry brandy

The candy flavor is there, but I'm not so sure about the apple.

CAPE CODDER

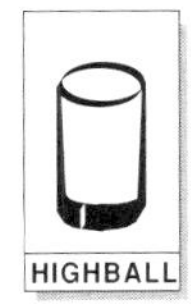

Build

1 1/4 oz vodka

Fill with cranberry juice

Not just for Thanksgiving.

CHAMPAGNE COCKTAIL

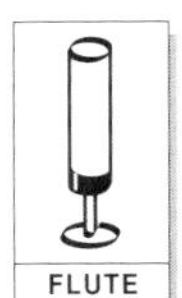

In a champagne glass

1/2 tsp sugar
1 dash Angostura bitters

Fill with champagne

Garnish with a lemon twist

Mix this carefully, the bitters make the champagne foam up.

CHAMPAGNE KIR

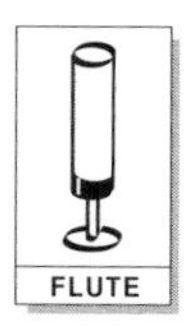

In a champagne glass

Fill with champagne
Add 1/2 oz creme de cassis

Garnish with a lemon twist

A fancy version of the Kir.

CHI CHI

Blend and serve frozen

1 1/4 oz vodka
1 3/4 oz pineapple juice
1 oz coconut syrup

Garnish with a flag or pineapple wedge

A piña colada with vodka instead of rum.

CHICAGO COFFEE

In a warmed mug

3/4 oz Cointreau
3/4 oz Kahlua

Fill with coffee
Top with whipped cream

I have no idea why this was named after Chicago.

CLARK BAR

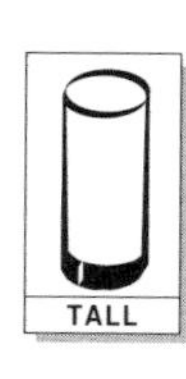

Build

3/4 oz Amaretto
3/4 oz dark creme de cacao

Fill with orange juice

Another candy drink. This will do more than give you cavities.

COLLINS (TOM, JOHN, ETC.)

Build

1 1/4 oz	**liquor**
2 oz	**bar sour**

Fill with 7 Up or Sprite

Garnish with a flag

Meet the family: Tom Collins is made with gin, John with bourbon, Joe with scotch (some say brandy), and the Vodka Collins is made with, uh, let me see...

COLORADO BULLDOG

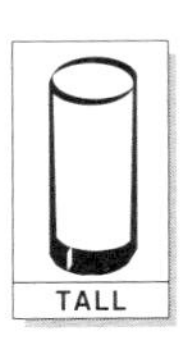

Build

1 1/4 oz	**vodka**
3/4 oz	**Kahlua**
1/2 oz	**half and half**

Splash of cola

Nice dog.

COWGIRL

Blend and strain

1 1/4 oz	**bourbon**
3/4 oz	**half and half**
1/2 tbs	**honey**

Use a blender or shake it like hell.

CREAMY MOTHER

Blend and strain

1/2 oz	**Kahlua**
1/2 oz	**dark creme de cacao**
1/2 oz	**vodka**
1/2 oz	**Galliano**
1/2 oz	**half and half**

HERE SHE COMES. (COWBOY TOAST)

CUBA LIBRE

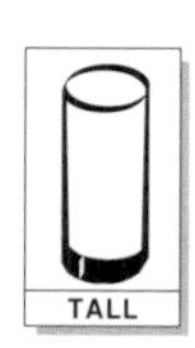

Build

1 1/4 oz rum

Fill with cola

Garnish with a lime wedge

This is different from a "Rum and Coke", which is served in a regular highball glass without the lime.

DAIQUIRI

Blend and serve frozen

1 1/2 oz rum
3 oz bar sour

This drink used to be shaken and strained, but people prefer slushy drinks these days.

DEATH IN THE AFTERNOON

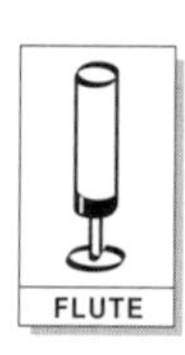

In a champagne glass

1 1/4 oz Pernod

Fill with champagne

This drink was invented for Ernest Hemingway, and named for his famous book on bullfighting.

DEEP THROAT

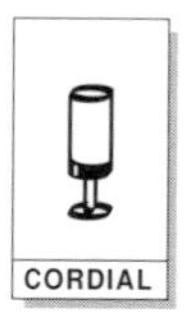

Float

1/3 Tia Maria
1/3 vodka
1/3 whipped cream

DIRTY MOTHER (GENTLE BULL)

Build

1 1/2 oz tequila
3/4 oz Kahlua
3/4 oz half and half

The name "Gentle Bull" is preferred in the more politically correct regions of our country.

DREAMSICLE

Blend and strain

1 1/4 oz Amaretto
2 oz orange juice
1 oz half and half

Sweet dreams!

DUBONNET COCKTAIL

Stir and strain

3/4 oz Dubonnet
3/4 oz gin

Garnish with a lemon twist

EVERYBODY'S IRISH COCKTAIL

Build

1 1/4 oz Irish whiskey
1 splash green creme de menthe
2 splashes Green Chartreuse

Garnish with a green olive

FIFTY FIFTY COCKTAIL

COCKTAIL

Stir and strain

3/4 oz gin
3/4 oz dry vermouth

This could be considered a martini. For more versions check out the martini section in this book.

FREDDIE FUDPUCKER

Build

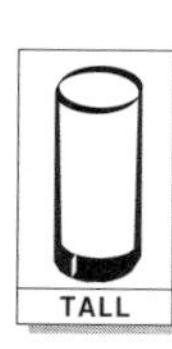
TALL

1 1/4 oz tequila

Fill with orange juice
Float Galliano

Garnish with a flag

Freddie is a close relative of the Wallbanger family.

FRENCH 75

Build

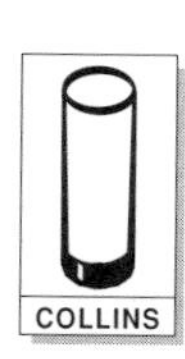
COLLINS

1 1/4 oz brandy
1 oz bar sour

Fill with champagne

Garnish with lemon twist

Named for a famous artillery piece used during World War One.

FRENCH CONNECTION

Build

ROCKS

1 1/2 oz Cognac or brandy
3/4 oz Amaretto

Also good served in a snifter.

FRENCH KISS

Build

3/4 oz	sweet vermouth
3/4 oz	dry vermouth

This is sort of a martini without the gin, the olive, the kick...

FUNKY MONKEY

Build

3/4 oz	rum
3/4 oz	creme de banana

Splash of orange juice

FUZZY NAVEL

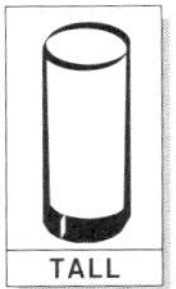

Build

1 1/4 oz peach schnapps

Fill with orange juice

This was not named for anyone I know.

FUZZY RICHARD

In a warmed mug

1/2 oz	Gran Marnier
1/2 oz	dark creme de cacao
1/2 oz	Kahlua

Fill with coffee
Top with whipped cream

GATES (COFFEE GATES)

In a warmed mug

1/2 oz	Tia Maria
1/2 oz	Gran Marnier
1/2 oz	dark creme de cacao

Fill with coffee
Top with whipped cream

GIN BUCK

Build

1 1/4 oz gin

Fill with ginger ale

Garnish with a lime wedge

A splash of sweetened lime juice will make this even better.

GIN FIZZ

Blend and strain over ice

1 1/4 oz	gin
1 oz	bar sour

Fill with soda

GIN SLING

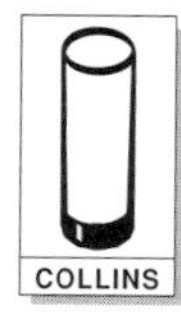

Build

3/4 oz	gin
1 1/2 oz	cherry brandy
1 oz	bar sour

Fill with soda
Float some B&B liqueur

Garnish with an orange slice

This is a good one, similar to the Singapore Sling.

GIN RICKEY

Build

1 1/4 oz gin

Juice of 1/2 lime
Fill with soda

Garnish with lime

This oldy is regaining popularity.

GIN AND TONIC

Build

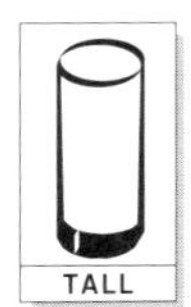

1 1/4 oz gin

Fill with tonic water

Garnish with a lime wedge

A classic, always good on a hot summer day.

GIRL SCOUT COOKIE

Blend and strain

3/4 oz Kahlua
3/4 oz peppermint schnapps
3/4 oz half and half

GODFATHER

Build

1 1/2 oz scotch
3/4 oz Amaretto

GODMOTHER

Build

1 1/2 oz vodka
3/4 oz Amaretto

What a christening that must have been!

GOLDEN CADILLAC

Blend and strain

3/4 oz light creme de cacao
3/4 oz half and half
3/4 oz Galliano

This one used to be garnished with big tail fins.

GOLDEN DREAM

Blend and strain

1 oz Galliano
1/2 oz triple sec
1/2 oz orange juice
1 oz half and half

GOLDEN FIZZ

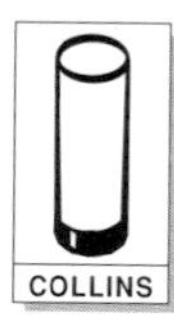

Blend and strain

1 egg yolk
1 1/2 oz gin
1 oz bar sour
2 oz half and half

Strain into glass
Fill with soda

GOOD AND PLENTY

Build

3/4 oz anisette or ouzo
3/4 oz Kahlua

They say that this tastes just like the candy of the same name.

GRASSHOPPER

Blend and strain

3/4 oz green creme de menthe
3/4 oz light creme de cacao
3/4 oz half and half

Substitute vanilla ice cream for the 1/2 & 1/2 for a real treat.

GREYHOUND

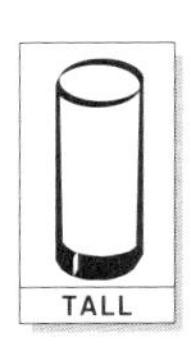

Build

1 1/4 oz vodka

Fill with grapefruit juice

A salty dog without the salt.

HARVEY FUNK (CHARLIE WALLBANGER)

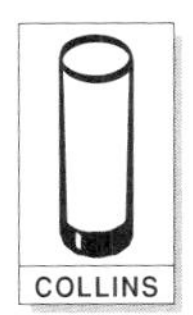

Build

1 1/4 oz rum

Fill with orange juice
Float Galliano liqueur

Garnish with a flag

AND REAL PAINS FOR OUR SHAM FRIENDS.

HARVEY WALLBANGER

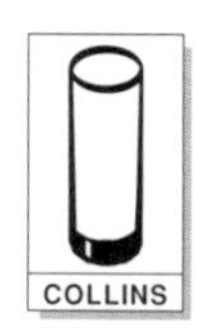

Build

1 1/4 oz vodka

Fill with orange juice
Float a little Galliano liqueur

Garnish with a flag

A dash of half and half stirred into this drink will make it real good.

HOT BUTTERED RUM

In a warmed mug

1 1/4 oz light rum
1 tbs buttered rum mix

Fill with hot water

Garnish with pat of butter and/or nutmeg

Check out the "Mixes" section for a hot buttered rum batter recipe.

HOT TODDY

In a warmed mug

1 1/4 oz brandy or bourbon
1 tsp sugar

Dissolve sugar in a mug with few drops of hot water. Add brandy, pour in boiling water

Garnish with a lemon twist or sprinkle with nutmeg

Honey is often substituted for the sugar.

HUGGY BEAR

In a warmed mug

3/4 oz Bailey's
3/4 oz Tuaca

Fill with coffee
Whipped cream is optional

IRISH COFFEE

In a warmed mug

1 tsp sugar
1 1/2 oz Irish whiskey

Fill with coffee
Top with whipped cream

Don't overpour the whiskey, you'll upset the delicate balance that St. Patrick enjoyed so.

INTERNATIONAL STINGER

Build

1 1/2 oz Metaxa
1 1/2 oz Galliano

Known by some as the Greco-Roman Stinger (by a few, anyway).

JACK ROSE

Blend and strain

1 1/4 oz apple brandy
3/4 oz sour
1 tsp grenadine

Apple brandy is also known as applejack, which explains the name of this one.

JOLLY RANCHER

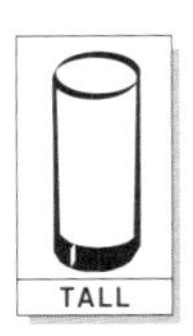

Build

3/4 oz apple schnapps
3/4 oz peach schnapps

Fill with cranberry juice

JAMAICAN COFFEE (CARIBBEAN COFFEE)

In a warmed mug

3/4 oz Tia Maria
3/4 oz dark rum

Fill with coffee
Top with whipped cream

JELLY BEAN

Float in order or build

1 oz anisette
1/2 oz sloe gin

Garnish with real jelly beans.

KAHLUA AND COFFEE

In a warmed mug

1 1/4 oz Kahlua

Fill with coffee
Top with whipped cream

KAMIKAZE

Stir and strain

1 1/4 oz vodka
3/4 oz triple sec
1/2 oz sweetened lime juice

Good before a surprise attack.

KEOKE COFFEE

In a warmed mug

1/2 oz dark creme de cacao
1/2 oz Kahlua
1/2 oz brandy

Fill with coffee
Top with whipped cream

KING ALPHONSE (BROWN COW)

Build

1 oz dark creme de cacao
1/2 oz half and half

How now, King Al?

KIR

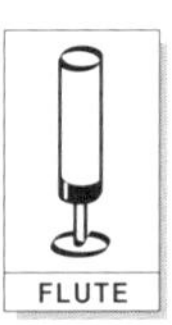

With or without ice

Chablis
1/2 oz creme de cassis

Garnish with a lemon twist

KOOLAID

Build

3/4 oz Amaretto
3/4 oz Midori

Splash of cranberry juice
Splash of orange juice

Garnish with a gummy worm in the bottom of the glass.

LONG ISLAND ICED TEA

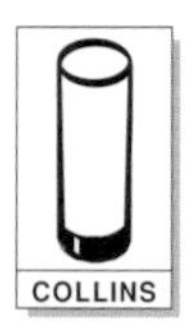

Build

1/2 oz rum
1/2 oz gin
1/2 oz vodka
1/2 oz triple sec

Splash of cola
Fill with bar sour

Garnish with lemon or lime wedge

These go down fast, and so will you. Be careful!

MADRAS

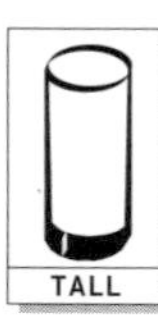

Build

1 1/4 oz vodka

Fill with: 1/2 orange juice
1/2 cranberry juice

MAI TAI

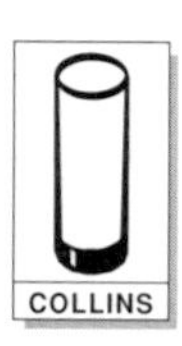

Build

1 1/4 oz light rum

Fill with: 3/4 pineapple juice
1/4 orange juice

Splash bar sour
Splash of grenadine
Float 1/2 oz dark rum

Garnish with a flag or a pineapple wedge

A commercial Mai Tai mix with rum is much easier, and tastes just as good.

MARGARITA

Blend and serve frozen in a glass with salted rim

1 1/4 oz tequila
3/4 oz triple sec
3 oz bar sour

Substitute gold tequila and Cointreau to make a Gold Coin.

COCKTAILS

MATADOR

Blend and strain

1 1/4 oz	**tequila**
2 oz	**pineapple juice**
1 oz	**sweetened lime juice**
1/2 oz	**grenadine**

It's a killer.

MELON BALL

Blend and strain

3/4 oz	**vodka**
3/4 oz	**Midori**
1 1/2 oz	**pineapple juice**

Garnish with a cherry

MEXICAN COFFEE

In a warmed mug

3/4 oz	**tequila**
3/4 oz	**Kahlua**

Fill with coffee
Top with whipped cream

MINT JULEP

Build

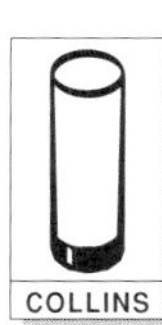

1 1/4 oz	**bourbon**
1 tsp	**sugar**
2-3 sprigs mint	

Muddle mint, sugar,
and 2 tsps water
Fill with crushed ice
and cold bourbon

Garnish with mint sprig

Everyone has their own "right" way of making this...it's always the same ingredients, but the rituals differ.

OLD WINE AND YOUNG WOMEN.

MISTS

Pack glass with crushed ice

1 1/2 oz any liquor

MIMOSA

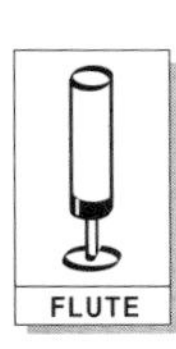

In a champagne glass

1/2 champagne
1/2 orange juice

This is why so many people like Sunday brunch.

MOOSE MILK

Build

1 1/4 oz bourbon

Fill with milk

1 1/4 oz Kahlua (optional)

Made popular by the ulcer crowd.

MOSCOW MOOSE

Build

3/4 oz peppermint schnapps
1/2 oz vodka

MOSCOW MULE

Build in a copper, pewter or glass mug

1 1/4 oz vodka

Fill with ginger beer

Garnish with lime wedge

Most bars don't stock ginger beer anymore.

MUDSLIDE (RUSSIAN CREAM, RUSSIAN REVOLUTION)

Build

3/4 oz Bailey's Irish Cream
1 1/2 oz Stolychnaya vodka

NEGRONI

Build

1/2 oz gin
1/2 oz sweet vermouth
1/2 oz Campari

Garnish with a twist

NUDGE

In a warmed mug

3/4 oz brandy
3/4 oz dark creme de cacao

Fill with coffee
Top with whipped cream

AND GOES TO BED MELLOW,

NUTTY ANGEL

Blend and strain

3/4 oz Frangelico
3/4 oz dark creme de cacao
3/4 oz half and half

Try substituting Kahlua for the creme de cacao.

OLD FASHIONED

Into empty glass

2 tsps sugar
2 dashes Angostura bitters
1/2 oz soda water

Muddle with lemon twist
Add ice and 1 1/4 oz bourbon

Garnish with a flag

To make a Sazerac pour some anisette into glass and swish around to coat, pour out and proceed with Old Fashioned recipe.

ORANGE BLOSSOM

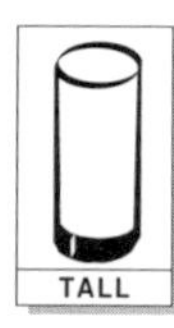

Blend and strain over ice

1 1/4 oz gin
1 1/2 oz orange juice
1/2 tsp sugar

PAINT THINNER

In a warmed mug

3/4 oz Bailey's
3/4 oz Dark rum

Fill with hot coffee

Sounds good, doesn't it?

PATTY MINT

Build

3/4 oz white creme de menthe
3/4 oz white creme de cacao

PEACHES AND CREAM

Build

1 1/4 oz peach schnapps
3/4 oz Bailey's Irish Cream
3/4 oz half and half

PEPPERMINT PATTY (SNUGGLER, SNOWBIRD, WHITE BIRD, BROKEN LEG)

In a warmed mug

1 1/4 oz peppermint schnapps

Fill with hot chocolate
Top with whipped cream

PEPTO BISMOL

Blend and strain

3/4 oz peppermint schnapps
3/4 oz Chambord
3/4 oz half and half

I think this would cause more discomfort than it would remedy.

AND DIES A HEARTY FELLOW.

PICON PUNCH (BASQUE PUNCH)

Build

Splash of grenadine
1 1/4 oz   Amer Picon

Fill with soda
Stir
Float a little brandy

Garnish with a twist

PIMM'S CUP COCKTAIL

Build

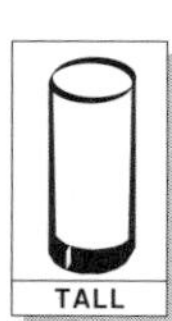

1 1/4 oz   Pimm's cup

Fill with 7 Up or soda

Garnish with a lemon twist

Garnish with a cucumber slice or stick if you can find one.

PIÑA COLADA

Blend and serve frozen

1 1/4 oz   rum
3 oz   pineapple juice
1 oz   coconut syrup

Garnish with a flag
or a pineapple wedge

PINK LADY

Blend and strain

1 1/4 oz   gin
1 oz   bar sour
1 oz   half and half
1/2 oz   grenadine

This used to be one popular drink.

PINK SQUIRREL

Blend and strain

3/4 oz Creme de Noyaux
3/4 oz light creme de cacao
3/4 oz half and half

This still pops up from time to time.

PLANTER'S PUNCH

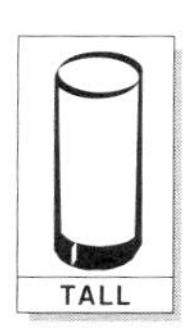

Blend and strain over ice

11/2 oz dark rum
1 oz bar sour
1 oz orange juice

Splash grenadine

Garnish with a flag

POUSSE CAFE

Float in layers in cordial glass

1/6 grenadine
1/6 white creme de menthe
1/6 green Chartreuse
1/6 dark creme de cacao
1/6 apricot brandy
1/6 brandy

It takes some effort to make this one.

PRESBYTERIAN

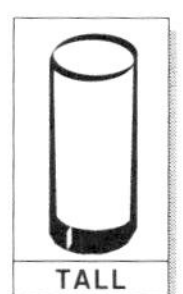

Build

1 1/4 oz bourbon

Fill with: 1/2 ginger ale
1/2 club soda

All denominations are welcome to try it.

PRESS

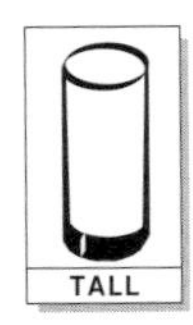

Build

1 1/4 oz bourbon
1/2 7 Up
1/2 club soda

RAMOS FIZZ

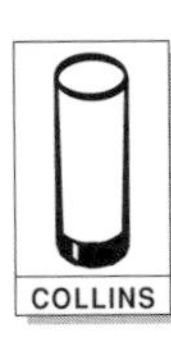

Blend and strain

1 egg white
1 1/4 oz gin (or vodka)
1 oz bar sour
2 oz half and half
1 tsp sugar
2 dashes Orange Flower Water
splash orange juice and/or triple sec (optional)

After straining into glass fill with soda water

A great morning after drink. Actually, it would be a decent breakfast.

ROCKY MOUNTAIN ROOT BEER

Build

1 oz vodka
1/2 oz Galliano

Fill with cola

ROOT BEER FLOAT

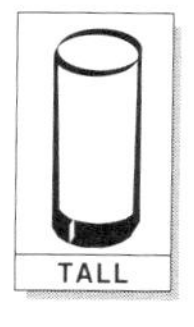

Build

1/2 oz	Galliano
3/4 oz	dark creme de cacao (or Kahlua)
1 oz	half and half
1 oz	cola

Not A & W, but it will do.

ROYAL FIZZ

Made just like a RAMOS FIZZ using a whole egg instead of just the white.

RUNNY NOSE

Build

1 1/4 oz Wild Turkey

Float white creme de menthe

Reminds me of a little kid I once knew.

RUSSIAN COFFEE

Blend and strain

3/4 oz	vodka
3/4 oz	Kahlua
3/4 oz	half and half

FOR WHEN WE'RE DEAD, WE'RE DEAD ALL OVER.

RUSSIAN MONK

Stir and strain or serve on the rocks

1 1/2 oz Stolychnaya vodka
3/4 oz Frangelico

RUSSIAN QUAALUDE

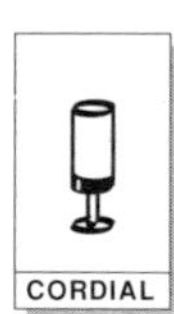

Float in order

1/2 oz Frangelico
1/2 oz vodka
1/2 oz half and half

Another Pousse Cafe.

RUSTY NAIL

Build

1 1/2 oz scotch
3/4 oz Drambuie

Try not to get bent.

SALTY DOG

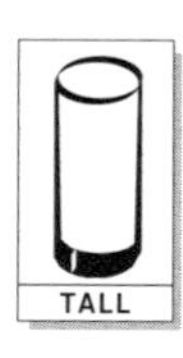

Build in salt rimmed glass

1 1/4 oz vodka

Fill with: grapefruit juice

If you forget the salt on the rim, the drink's name changes to Greyhound or sometimes Bulldog.

SAGE (SAGE BRUSH)

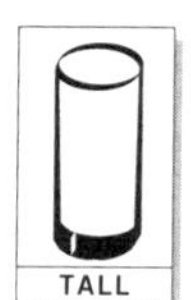

Build

1 1/4 oz bourbon

Fill with: 1/2 7 Up
 1/2 water

Garnish with a lemon twist

SCARLET O'HARA

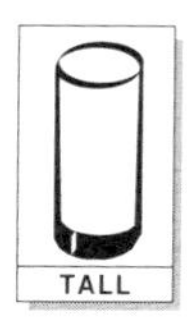

Build

1 1/4 oz Southern Comfort

Fill with cranberry juice

SCOTCH COFFEE

In a coffee mug

1 1/4 oz Drambuie

Fill with coffee
Top with whipped cream

SCREAMING ORGASM #1

Build

1/2 oz Gran Marnier
1/2 oz Bailey's Irish Cream
1/2 oz Amaretto

Fill with soda water

Some people call this series of drinks "S. O.'s".

A QUICK DEATH AND A HAPPY ONE,

SCREAMING ORGASM #2

Build

1 1/2 oz vodka
3/4 oz Kahlua
3/4 oz Bailey's Irish Cream

SCREAMING ORGASM #3

In a coffee mug

3/4 oz Gran Marnier
3/4 oz Bailey's Irish Cream

Fill with hot water (or coffee)

SCREWDRIVER

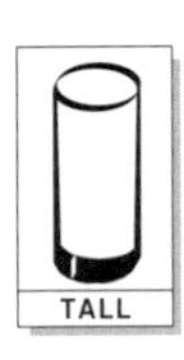

Build

1 1/4 oz vodka

Fill with orange juice

A very useful tool.

SEABREEZE

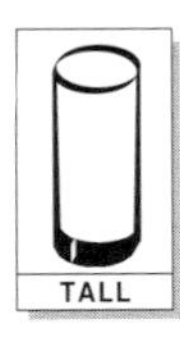

Build

1 1/4 oz vodka

Fill with cranberry and grapefruit juices

SEPARATOR

Build

1 1/2 oz brandy
3/4 oz Kahlua
3/4 oz half and half

SEX ON THE BEACH

Blend and strain

3/4 oz Chambord
3/4 oz Midori

Splash bar sour
Splash pineapple juice

Swimming suits are optional.

SHANDY GAFF

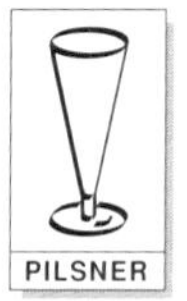

Mix

5 oz beer
5 oz ginger ale

This will anger both beer lovers and ginger ale fans.

SHINY NAVEL

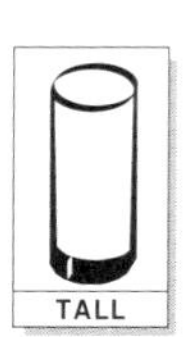

Build

1 1/4 oz apple schnapps

Fill with orange juice

Garnish with a flag

SICILIAN KISS

CORDIAL

Float in order

3/4 oz	Amaretto
3/4 oz	Southern Comfort

SICILIAN KISS COCKTAIL

COCKTAIL

Blend and strain

3/4 oz	Amaretto
3/4 oz	Southern comfort
3/4 oz	half and half

SIDECAR

COCKTAIL

Blend and strain into a glass with a sugared rim

1 1/4 oz	brandy
3/4 oz	triple sec
3 oz	bar sour

An oldy but a goldy...try it!

SILVER FIZZ

COCKTAIL

Blend and strain

1	egg white
1 1/2 oz	gin
1 oz	bar sour
2 oz	half and half

Strain into glass then fill with soda

SILVER FOX (VELVET HAMMER)

Blend and strain

3/4 oz triple sec
3/4 oz light creme de cacao
3/4 oz half and half

Hey bartender, hit me again!

SINGAPORE SLING

Build

COLLINS

1 1/4 oz gin

Fill with: 1/2 7 Up
1/2 bar sour
Float cherry brandy
Splash grenadine (optional)

Garnish with a lime

SKIP AND GO NAKED

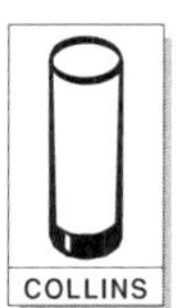

Build

1 1/4 oz gin
1 oz bar sour

Dash grenadine
Fill with beer

Garnish with lime wedge

It would take several of these before I would even consider it.

SLOE COMFORTABLE SCREW

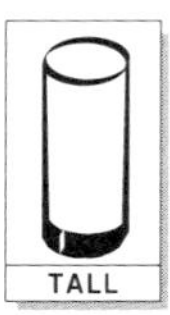

Build

3/4 oz sloe gin
3/4 oz Southern Comfort

Fill with orange juice

FOR TOMORROW WE MAY DIE.

SLOE COMFORTABLE SCREW UP AGAINST THE WALL

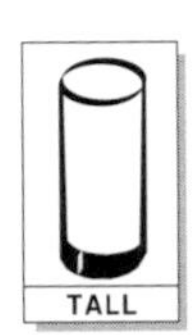

Build

3/4 oz sloe gin
3/4 oz Southern Comfort

Fill with orange juice
Float Galliano

I think someone came up with the name first, and concocted the drink to fit it.

SLOE GIN FIZZ

Blend and strain

1 1/4 oz sloe gin
2 oz bar sour

Strain into glass, then fill with soda

Don't forget the soda, that's what makes it fizz.

SLOE SCREW (COBRA)

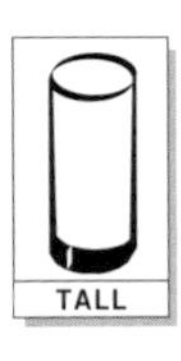

Build

1 1/2 oz sloe gin

Fill with orange juice

SMITH AND KEARNS

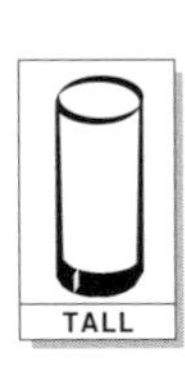

Build

1 1/4 oz dark creme de cacao
1 oz half and half

Fill with soda

Many bartenders will substitute cola for the soda.

MAN LEARNS TO CLIMB,

SNAKE BITE

Build

1 1/4 oz Yukon Jack

Float sweetened lime juice

SNOW SHOE

Build

1 1/4 oz Wild Turkey

Float peppermint schnapps

SOURS

Blend and strain

1 1/4 oz bourbon
(or any liquor)
3 oz bar sour

Garnish with a cherry

Amaretto makes a great sour, give it a try.

SPANISH COFFEE

In a coffee mug

3/4 oz brandy
3/4 oz Kahlua

Fill with coffee
Top with whipped cream

Sí señor, este café es buenísimo.

NOT WHILE HE STOPS TO PRAY,

SPRITZER

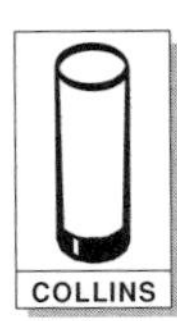

Build

Fill with: 1/2 Chablis
1/2 club soda

Garnish with a twist or lime wedge

STONE SOUR

Blend and strain

1 1/4 oz bourbon (or any liquor)
1 1/2 oz bar sour
1 1/2 oz orange juice

Garnish with a cherry

STARBOARD LIGHT

Build

1 1/2 oz gin
3/4 oz green creme de menthe

Port is left, starboard right, port is left, starboard right...

STINGER

Build

1 1/2 oz brandy
3/4 oz white creme de menthe

STRAWBERRY DAIQUIRI

Blend and serve frozen

1 1/2 oz	**light rum**
3 oz	**bar sour**
3 oz	**fresh or frozen strawberries**

Dash grenadine

Add a dash of anisette to this for a surprisingly tasty cocktail.

STRAWBERRY MARGARITA

Follow recipe for Margarita, and add fresh or frozen strawberries before blending

Try any fresh fruit in place of strawberries for this and the Daiquiri.

SUNRISE COLADA

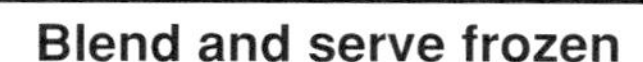

Blend and serve frozen

1 1/4 oz	**rum**
3 oz	**orange juice**
1 oz	**coconut syrup**

Garnish with a flag or pineapple wedge

SUNSET

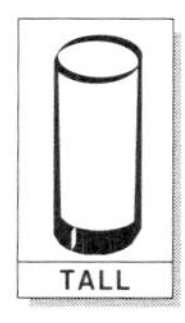

Build

1 1/4 oz tequila

Fill with orange juice
Float sloe gin

Garnish with a cherry

Brandy in place of tequila will turn this into a California Sunset.

SWAMPWATER

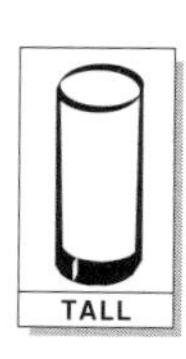

Build

1 1/4 oz green Chartreuse

Fill with pineapple juice

Garnish with a lime wedge

Not a well known drink, probably for good reason.

TEQUILA SUNRISE

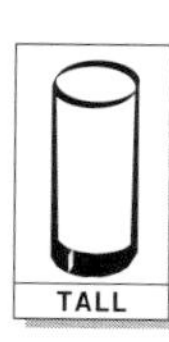

Build

1 1/4 oz tequila

Fill with orange juice
Float grenadine

Garnish with a cherry

Be sure to check their ID's.

THICK MICK

Build

3/4 oz Irish whiskey
1/2 oz Irish Mist

TIA BEATRIZ

Blend and strain

1 oz Tia Maria liqueur
1/2 oz anisette
1 1/2 oz half and half

My original recipe and a winner in a contest a few years ago.

TOM COLLINS

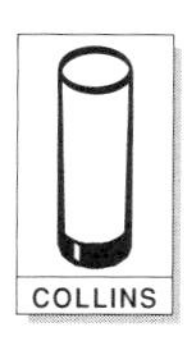

Build

1 1/4 oz	gin
2 oz	bar sour

Fill with 7 Up

Garnish with a flag

Those bars that have it use crushed ice in all Collins.

TOOTIE FRUITY LIFESAVER

Blend and strain

1/2 oz	Galliano
1 1/4 oz	creme de banana
1 oz	cranberry juice
1 oz	orange juice
1 oz	pineapple juice

Garnish with a flag

TOOTSIE ROLL

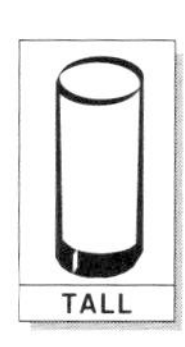

Build

1 1/4 oz	dark creme de cacao

Fill with orange juice

So what would you add to this to make a Tootsie Roll Pop?

TOPAZ

Blend and strain

1/2 oz	vodka
1/2 oz	Galliano
1 oz	Gran Marnier
2 oz	orange juice

TRANSFUSION

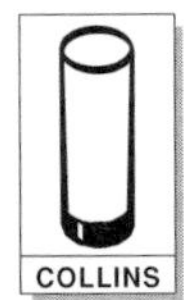

Build

1 1/4 oz vodka

Fill with grape juice
Splash soda

VELVET FONDABINIE

Blend and strain

1 1/4 oz	**Kahlua**
2 oz	**orange juice**
1 oz	**half and half**

They say all the best fondabinies are made of velvet.

VELVET GLOVE

Blend and strain

3/4 oz	**dark creme de cacao**
3/4 oz	**vodka**
3/4 oz	**half and half**

WARD EIGHT

Blend and strain into crushed ice

1 1/4 oz	**whiskey**
1 oz	**bar sour**
1 tsp	**grenadine**

Garnish with a flag

CANDY IS DANDY,

WHITE CADILLAC

Blend and strain

3/4 oz half and half
3/4 oz triple sec
3/4 oz Galliano

WHITE CORAL

Blend and strain

3/4 oz Kahlua
3/4 oz Cointreau
3/4 oz half and half

WHITE LIGHTNING

Build

1 1/2 oz vodka
3/4 oz light creme de cacao

Not the moonshiner's version.

WHITE RUSSIAN

Build

1 1/2 oz vodka
3/4 oz Kahlua
3/4 oz half and half

BUT LIQUOR IS QUICKER.

WINE COOLER

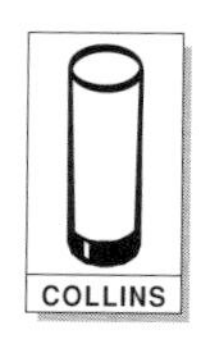

Build

Fill with: 1/2 Chablis
1/2 7 Up or Sprite

Garnish with lemon twist or lime wedge

Use an inexpensive wine for this recipe.

WINDJAMMER

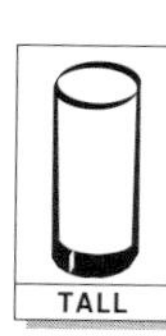

Build

1 1/4 oz vodka

Fill with: 1/2 orange juice
1/2 grapefruit juice

WINNEMUCCA COFFEE

In a coffee mug

3/4 oz anisette
3/4 oz brandy
1 tsp sugar

Fill with hot coffee

Popular in Nevada and Northern California.

WOO WOO

Blend and strain

1 1/4 oz vodka
1/2 oz peach schnapps
3 oz cranberry juice

YELLOW CANARY

Blend and strain

1 1/4 oz	vodka
3/4 oz	creme de banana
1 oz	orange juice
1 oz	pineapple juice

YOUR NEIGHBOR'S WIFE

Blend and strain or build

1 1/4 oz	cherry brandy
3 oz	sour

Splash grenadine

ZOMBIE

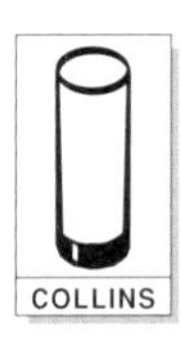

Build

1 oz	light rum
1/2 oz	amber rum
1/2 oz	Jamaican rum
1 oz	sweetened lime juice
1 oz	pineapple juice
1/2 oz	grenadine

Float 3/4 oz "151" rum

Garnish with a flag

ACAPULCO COCKTAIL

Stir and strain

1 1/4 oz light rum
1 tbs triple sec
1 tbs sweetened lime juice

CAIPIRINHA

Into an empty glass

4 lime wedges
1 tbs simple syrup

Muddle well, then add

1 1/4 oz light rum

COSMOPOLITAN

Blend and strain

1 1/4 oz citrus vodka
1 tbs triple sec
1 tbs cranberry juice
1 tbs fresh lime juice

EL PRESIDENTE

Blend and strain

1 1/4 oz light rum
1 tbs fresh lime juice
1 tbs pineapple juice
Splash grenadine

HERE'S TO A CLEAR CONSCIENCE - OR A POOR MEMORY.

FIXES

Into an empty glass

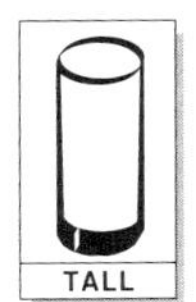

1 1/4 oz	gin, rum or whiskey
1 oz	bar sour
Splash	water

Use half brandy and half cherry brandy for a Brandy Fix

Fill with crushed ice

Garnish with a flag

HAVANA COCKTAIL

Blend and strain

1 1/4 oz	light rum
1 tbs	pineapple juice
1 tbs	fresh lemon juice

LEMON DROP

Stir and strain into a cocktail glass with a sugared rim

1 1/4 oz	citrus vodka
1 tbs	triple sec

METROPOLITAN

Blend and strain

1 1/4 oz	currant vodka
Splash	sweetened lime juice
Splash	fresh lime juice
Splash	cranberry juice

Garnish with a lime wedge

MIND ERASER

Float in layers in a cordial glass

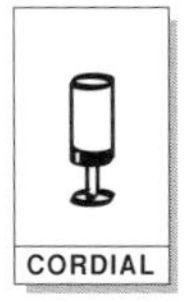

1 1/2 tbs Kahlua
1 1/2 tbs vodka
1 1/2 tbs soda

Drink from the bottom up

One short straw

MOJITO

Into an empty glass

6 fresh mint leaves
1 tbs simple syrup
1 tbs fresh lime juice

Muddle well, then add

1 1/4 oz light rum
1 1/4 oz soda

Garnish with a lime wedge

MONKEY GLAND

Blend and strain

1 1/4 oz gin
1 tbs benedictine
2 tbs orange juice
Splash grenadine

PIERCED NAVEL

Build

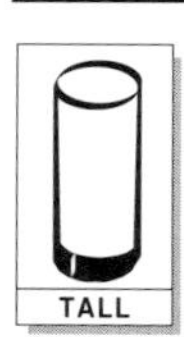

1 1/4 oz peach schnapps

Fill with cranberry juice

LAUGH AND THE WORLD LAUGHS WITH YOU;

PISCO SOUR

Blend and strain

1	egg white
1 1/4 oz	Pisco brandy
1 1/2 oz	bar sour
2 dashes	Angostura bitters

SCORPION

Blend and strain over ice

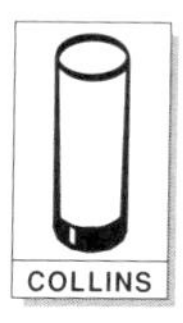

1 1/4 oz	dark rum
1 tbs	brandy
1 tbs	dry vermouth
2 tbs	orange juice
2 tbs	lemon juice
1 tsp	orgeat syrup

Garnish with a sprigg of mint

VERMOUTH CASSIS

Build

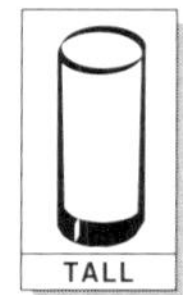

2 oz	dry vermouth
1 tbs	creme de cassis

Fill with soda

Garnish with a twist

YELLOWBIRD

Blend and strain

1 1/4 oz	light rum
1 tbs	Galliano
1 tbs	triple sec
1 tbs	fresh lime juice

MARTINIS

The martini is reputed to be the most famous and the most popular cocktail in the world. Like jazz, it is distinctly American in origin. Yet there is little agreement on just when and where in America it was invented. Three of the more believable versions of how it got its name follow:

Some say it was invented by Professor Jerry Thomas, the famous bartender and author of the 1864 book "The Bon Vivant's Companion, or How To Mix Drinks", which did much to popularize the cocktail. While working at a bar in the gold fields of California, he concocted a "special drink" at the request of a customer who was on his way to ... Martinez, California.

Others claim that the inventor was a less renowned but well-loved bartender named Martini who worked at Delmonico's in New York City.

And some with still less imagination say that the cocktail's name stems from a brand of vermouth used in the elaboration of the drink, Martini and Rossi.

All martini lovers seem to agree that as a cocktail, the martini cannot be improved upon. Yet, as in jazz, invention and improvisation are the norm. A little study turns up scores of martini recipes which have been developed through the years. The precursor was the Manhattan, the archetypal short drink, called by one author "the concentrated essence of life", not at all like the taller and more elaborate long drinks. You will see the similarities between the Manhattan and the original Martini in the excerpted recipes that follow.

Despite all the romance, tradition and ritual perpetuated by martini lovers, major changes appeared in the recipes, mirroring the tastes of the time. The martini became dry, then drier, to the extreme of leaving out the vermouth altogether. Garnish changed from cherry to the olive, to lemon peel and hot pepper and about anything that would fit into the glass. Vodka was sometimes substituted for gin, and most radical of all, it is now even served up on the rocks!

One aspect of the martini never changes, though. It must be served cold. So whether stirring or shaking, use lots of ice, and then more ice. And chill the glasses before adding the cocktail. But when it comes to ingredients, just remember, the customer is always right.

AND TO TELL YOU THE TRUTH IT IS NOT THE VERMOUT

Manhattan Cocktail

Fill mixing glass half-full fine ice, add two dashes gum syrup, two dashes Peyschaud or Angostura bitters, one half jigger Italian vermouth, one half jigger whiskey. Mix, strain into cocktail glass. Add a piece of lemon peel or a cherry.

Martini Cocktail

Half a mixing glass full fine ice, three dashes orange bitters, one half jigger Tom gin, one half jigger Italian vermouth, a piece of lemon peel. Mix, strain into cocktail glass. Add a maraschino cherry, if desired by customer.

(from Modern American Drinks, by George J. Kappeler, 1895)

DIRTY MARTINI

1 1/2 oz gin
A few drops of brine from the olive jar
Garnish with an olive

DRY MANHATTAN

1 1/2 oz bourbon
1/2 oz dry vermouth
Garnish with an olive

DRY MARTINI

1 1/2 oz gin
A few drops dry vermouth
Garnish with an olive

I THINK THAT PERHAPS IT'S THE GIN. (OGDEN NASH)

DRY ROB ROY

1 1/2 oz scotch
1/2 oz dry vermouth
Garnish with an olive

FINO MARTINI

1 1/2 oz gin
1/2 oz fino sherry
Garnish with an olive

GIBSON

1 1/2 oz gin
A few drops of dry vermouth
Garnish with a pearl onion

GIMLET

1 1/2 oz gin
3/4 oz sweetened lime juice
Garnish with a lime wedge

GIN AND IT

1 1/2 oz gin
1/2 oz sweet vermouth
Garnish with a lemon twist

A WOMAN DROVE ME TO DRINK, AND I NEVER EVEN

ITALIAN MARTINI

1 1/2 oz gin or vodka
Dash of anisette
Garnish with an olive

MANHATTAN

1 1/2 oz bourbon
1/2 oz sweet vermouth
Dash of Angostura bitters (optional)
Garnish with a cherry

MARTINEZ COCKTAIL

1 oz gin
1 oz sweet vermouth
Dash of Angostura bitters
Dash of simple syrup

MARTINI

1 1/2 oz gin
A few drops of dry vermouth
Garnish with an olive

NAKED MARTINI

1 1/2 oz gin
Garnish with an olive

WROTE A NOTE TO THANK HER. (W. C. FIELDS)

PAISLEY MARTINI

1 1/2 oz gin
1/4 oz dry vermouth
Dash of scotch

PERFECT MANHATTAN

1 1/2 oz bourbon
1/4 oz dry vermouth
1/4 oz sweet vermouth
Garnish with a lemon twist

PERFECT MARTINI

1 1/2 oz gin
1/4 oz dry vermouth
1/4 oz sweet vermouth
Garnish with an olive

PERFECT ROB ROY

1 1/2 oz scotch
1/4 oz dry vermouth
1/4 oz sweet vermouth
Garnish with a lemon twist

PINK GIN

1 1/2 oz gin
2 dashes Angostura bitters

I MUST GET OUT OF THESE WET CLOTHES AND

ROB ROY

1 1/2 oz scotch
1/2 oz sweet vermouth
Dash of Angostura bitters (optional)
Garnish with a cherry

SMOKY MARTINI (HARPER HOUSE)

1 1/2 oz gin
A few drops of scotch
Garnish with an olive

SWEET MARTINI

1 1/2 oz gin
1/2 oz sweet vermouth
Dash of Angostura bitters (optional)

VODKA GIBSON

1 1/2 oz vodka
A few drops of dry vermouth
Garnish with a pearl onion

VODKA GIMLET

1 1/2 oz vodka
3/4 oz sweetened lime juice
Garnish with a lime wedge

INTO A DRY MARTINI. (ALEXANDER WOOLLCOTT)

ALMOND ICED COFFEE

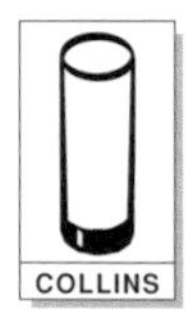

Build

1 cup	coffee
1 cup	milk
1/2 tsp	vanilla extract
1/4 tsp	almond extract
1 tsp	sugar

Sprinkle with cinnamon

BERRY YOGURT COOLER

Blend and freeze

1 cup	strawberries
1 cup	cranberry juice
1/2 cup	yogurt

COCO COLADA

Blend and strain

1 oz	creme de coconut
2 oz	pineapple juice

Fill with soda

FRULATTI DI FRUTTA

Blend and strain

1 cup	fresh fruit
2/3 cup	milk

Sugar to taste

IF YOU DRINK LIKE A FISH,

HOT SPICED FRUIT TEA

In a warmed mug

1 cup water
1 cup pineapple juice
4 cloves

Add: juice of 1 lemon
1 tbs sugar

LEMONADE OR LIMEADE SYRUP

Boil and cool

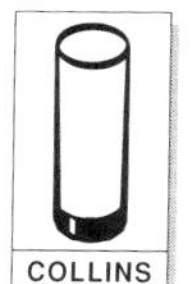

1 cup sugar
1 cup water

Add: 1 cup lemon or lime juice

Mix 3 tbs with 8 oz water or soda over ice

MAPLE SPRITZER

Build

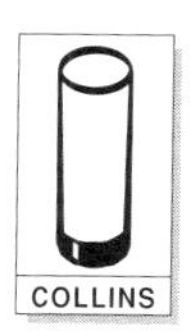

2 tbs maple syrup

Fill with soda

NEW YORK EGG CREAM

Blend without ice

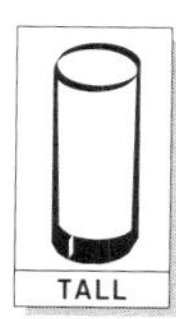

8 tbs chocolate or vanilla syrup
1 1/2 cups milk

Pour into glass and stir in soda water

ORANGE BANANA SMOOTHEE

Blend and freeze

1 banana
1 cup orange juice

ORANGE JULIUS

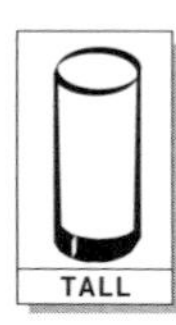

Blend and strain

3 oz orange juice
1 1/2 oz half and half

Fill with soda

QUEEN CHARLIE

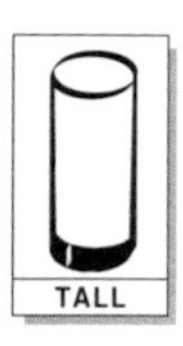

Build

Soda

Splash of grenadine

ROY ROGERS

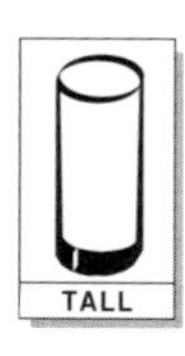

Build

Cola

Float grenadine

SHIRLEY TEMPLE

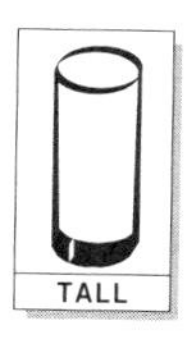

Build

7 Up or Sprite

Float grenadine

STRAWBERRY BANANA MILK

Blend and freeze

1 cup	strawberries
1	banana
1 cup	milk

TOMATO ORANGE COOLER

Build

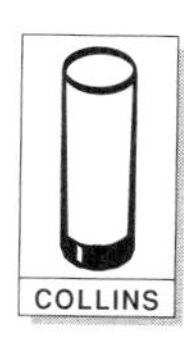

1 cup	tomato juice
1/2 cup	orange juice

Garnish with a twist and a fresh basil twig

TOMATO TONIC COOLER

Build

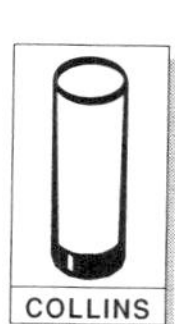

6 oz	tomato juice
1 1/2 tbs	lime juice

Top with tonic water

Garnish with a wheel

THE NUMBER OF MEN WHO THINK THEY CAN SING.

AMARETTO - A sweet liqueur flavored mainly with almonds and apricot kernels. The original and most popular Amaretto di Saronno is imported from Italy.

AMER PICON - Brand name of a French aperitif flavored with orange peels and gentian. It is syrupy with a bitter flavor.

ANISETTE - A sweet aniseed flavored liqueur.

APRICOT BRANDY - A sweetish apricot flavored liqueur.

BAILEY'S IRISH CREAM - A liqueur based on cream and Irish whiskey, made in Ireland.

BEER - An alcoholic beverage made from fermented grain.

BENEDICTINE - Brand name of an herbal liqueur invented by Benedictine monks in 1510.

BLACKBERRY BRANDY - A sweet blackberry flavored liqueur.

BLUE CURAÇAO - An orange flavored liqueur, also available in an orange color. It is drier and lower in alcohol than triple sec.

BOURBON - American whisky, named for Bourbon County, Kentucky, where it allegedly originated. By law it must be distilled from a mash containing at least 51% corn.

BRANDY - A spirit distilled from grape wine or other fruit ferments. Cognac is a grape brandy made in the Charante Province of France.

CAMPARI - An Italian aperitif with a bitter quinine flavor.

CHABLIS - A generic white wine usually from California named for a French wine district, often used as a house wine.

CHAMBORD - Is a magnificent liqueur made with rich framboises (small black raspberries) and other fruits and herbs combined with honey.

CHAMPAGNE - In the U.S., a generic term for sparkling (carbonated) wine. In Europe this name can only be used for the sparkling wines of the Champagne region of France.

CHERRY BRANDY - A sweet cherry flavored liqueur.

COINTREAU - Brand name of a high quality triple sec.

CREME DE BANANA - A sweet banana flavored liqueur.

CREME DE CACAO - A sweet liqueur flavored mainly with chocolate and vanilla, available in both white and dark versions.

CREME DE CASSIS - A sweet black currant flavored liqueur.

CREME DE MENTHE - A mint flavored liqueur available in both white and green versions.

CREME DE NOYAUX - A reddish, sweet liqueur flavored with almond.

DRAMBUIE - Brand name of an herb and honey flavored liqueur based on Scotch whiskey, made in Scotland.

DRY VERMOUTH - A dry, white fortified wine infused with many herbs and spices.

DUBONNET - Brand name of a French vermouth-style aperitif with a bittersweet flavor.

FRANGELICO - Brand name of a sweet hazelnut liqueur made in Italy.

GALLIANO - Brand name of a sweet herbal liqueur made in Italy.

GIN - A clear distilled spirit flavored with botanicals, the dominant flavor being juniper berries.

GRAN MARNIER - Brand name of a French orange flavored liqueur based on Cognac.

GREEN CHARTREUSE - A 110 proof herbal liqueur made by Carthusian monks in France. They also make a yellow version at a lower proof.

KAHLUA - Brand name of a coffee liqueur made in Mexico.

IRISH WHISKEY - This whiskey is made from several grains in addition to barley, triple distilled resulting in a smooth and mellow product.

METAXA - Brand name of an aromatic and slightly sweetened brandy made in Greece.

MIDORI - A Japanese honeydew flavored liqueur.

OUZO - A brandy based liqueur flavored with anise and licorice made in Greece.

PERNOD - Brand name of a dry aniseed liqueur made in France.

RUM - A spirit made by distilling fermented molasses, available in light and dark versions of various proofs.

SCHNAPPS - In Europe, a generic name for clear hard liquor. In the U.S. they are clear, sweet flavored liqueurs, the most popular being peppermint schnapps.

SCOTCH - Whisky made in Scotland. Its unique flavor comes from the smoke dried malt used in making the whiskey.

SLOE GIN - A liqueur made by macerating sloeberries in gin.

SOUTHERN COMFORT - Brand name of an American whisky.

SWEET VERMOUTH - A sweet red fortified wine infused with many herbs and spices.

TEQUILA - A Mexican spirit distilled from the agave cactus plant.

TIA MARIA - A coffee flavored liqueur based on rum and made in Jamaica.

TRIPLE SEC - A clear, sweet orange-flavored liqueur.

TUACA - A sweet Italian liqueur flavored with vanilla and other herbs.

WINE - An alcoholic beverage made from fermented fruit.

VODKA - A clear spirit of neutral flavor, distilled at 190 proof and brought down to 80 or 100 proof by addition of distilled water.

WILD TURKEY - Brand name of a high quality bourbon whiskey.

YUKON JACK - A citrus-herb liqueur based on blended whiskey and made in Canada.

BACK
Refers to a plain mixer, coffee, or beer served in a separate glass, along with an alcoholic drink served neat or on the rocks.

BITTERS
An aromatic blend of water and alcohol infused with herbs, roots, and other flavoring agents, the most popular being Angostura Bitters.

BLEND
To use an electric blender to mix cocktails containing cordials, sugar, eggs, half and half, etc. Most recipes that call for shaking are nowadays blended.

BUILD
To build a drink is to place all ingredients directly into the glass it is to be served in, rather than stirring or blending and straining into another glass.

CALL LIQUOR
Liquors requested by name, such as J&B scotch or Jack Daniel's whisky.

CHASER
Usually a beer served with a straight shot, although the term has been used for other drinks (usually plain) served on the side.

CORDIAL
Also called liqueurs. Spirits that are sweetened and flavored with herbs and/or fruit.

DITCH
Normally a bourbon and water, though one of my customers used to order "vodka ditches" or vodka and water.

86
To "86" a customer is to refuse to serve him (or her) because he is drunk or generally obnoxious.

FLAG
A garnish made by attaching a maraschino cherry to an orange slice with a toothpick.

FLAMED
To ignite a high proof liquor, either straight or floated on a cocktail, for a dramatic effect.

FLAMING SHOT
Also for dramatic effect. A straight shot is flamed and downed in one gulp, often resulting in singed facial hair and burned tonsils.

FLOAT
Pouring spirits carefully into a glass so they don't mix, to obtain a layered effect as in the Pousse Cafe, or as a finishing touch on cocktails like the Mai Tai.

FROST
1. To chill a glass by keeping it in a cooler or crushed ice.
2. To coat the rim of a glass with sugar.

FROZEN
A drink, usually a Margarita or a Daiquiri, blended with plenty of ice to achieve a thick slushy consistency. These are usually ordered when the bartender is very busy.

GARBAGE
Garnish; a "garbage drink" has many ingredients and often a lot of fruit garnish, most of which ends up in the bar's dump sink.

GARBAGE-TINI
A martini with olives, onions, lemon twists and sometimes even fruit garnish.

GARNISH
Refers to the fruits and foods used as a finishing touch on drinks, everything from cherries and celery to pickled beans.

GENERIC WINES
Wines named for their style rather than the type of grape used, example, Burgundy, Rosé and Chablis.

HIGH
Means mixed with whiskey, as in "seven high" (whiskey and 7 Up) and "water high" (whiskey and water).

HIGHBALL
A drink built with a liquor and any mix such as soda, cola or 7 Up.

LIQUEUR
Same as CORDIAL.

LIQUOR
A distilled alcoholic beverage; spirits.

MIX
Any non-alcoholic liquid that is mixed with liquor to make a drink.

MUDDLE
To blend ingredients, usually sugar, fruit and liquids, with a pestle (muddler) in the bottom of a glass before adding the mix.

NEAT
A liquor served undiluted with ice or mix, usually in a shot glass.

ON AND OVER
Means to blend a drink and then serve it over ice.

ON THE ROCKS
To serve a liquor with ice.

OVER
Same as ON THE ROCKS.

POUSSE CAFE
A drink consisting of liqueurs carefully floated to create a layered effect. These should not be downed in one gulp; however, people are calling the more recent versions of these SHOOTERS.

PROOF
A measure of alcohol content. In the United States 200 proof is the same as 100%. 86 proof would be 43% alcohol. Great Britain and Europe each have their own proof systems, but imported bottles are marked using the United States system.

ROCKS
A term meaning ICE CUBES.

SHAKE
To mix a drink by shaking with ice in a cocktail shaker. Very few do this nowadays, most preferring to use an electric blender.

SPLASH
A small amount of mix, as in a bourbon on the rocks with a splash of soda.

SQUEEZE
A lime or lemon wedge usually squeezed and dropped into a drink as garnish.

STIR AND STRAIN
A way to mix drinks and chill them without much dilution. Mainly used for Martinis and Manhattans.

TREE
Slang for the celery sticks used as garnish in Bloody Mary.

TWIST
A lemon peel, usually twisted over a drink to release its oil before dropping in as a garnish.

VARIETAL
A wine known by the major variety of grapes used in its production, like Cabernet Sauvignon or Chardonnay.

VIRGIN DRINKS
A cocktail made omitting the alcohol, such as a Virgin Bloody Mary or a Virgin Piña Colada.

WEDGE
Lemons and limes are cut into wedge shapes and used as garnish in many drinks, and are thus called "wedges".

WELL
Refers to the area near the ice bin where the WELL BRANDS or WELL STOCK (the house liquor) is kept.

WHEEL
Refers to lemons, limes or oranges cut in flat round slices and used to garnish cocktails

INDEX

BOURBON (cont.)

Perfect Manhattan
Presbyterian
Press
Sage
Sours
Stone Sour
Ward Eight

BRANDY

Angel's Wing
Benedictine and Brandy (B&B)
Between the Sheets
Brandy Alexander
Burras Peg (Cognac)
Cafe Frangelico
Cafe Royal
French 75
French Connection
Hot Toddy
Keoke Coffee
Nudge
Pousse Cafe
Separator
Sidecar
Spanish Coffee
Stinger
Winnemucca Coffee

CAMPARI

Americano
Campari and Soda
Negroni

CHAMBORD

Pepto Bismol
Sex on the Beach

CHAMPAGNE

Bellini
Burras Peg
Champagne Cocktail
Champagne Kir
Champagne Magnolia
Death in the Afternoon
French 75
Mimosa

CHERRY BRANDY

Candy Apple
Gin Sling
Singapore Sling
Your Neighbor's Wife

COFFEE DRINKS

Cafe Frangelico
Cafe International
Cafe Royal
Calypso Coffee
Chicago Coffee
Fuzzy Richard
Gates (Coffee Gates)
Irish Coffee
Jamaican Coffee (Caribbean Coffee)
Kahlua and Coffee
Keoke
Mexican Coffee
Nudge
Scotch Coffee
Spanish Coffee
Winnemucca Coffee

COINTREAU

Burras Peg
Chicago Coffee
White Coral

GALLIANO (cont.)

GIN

GIN (cont.)

GRAN MARNIER

GREEN CHARTREUSE

GREEN CREME DE MENTHE

IRISH MINT

IRISH WHISKEY

INDEX

RUM

Bacardi Cocktail
Bahama Mama
Banana Daiquiri
Between the Sheets
Blue Hawaiian
Calypso Coffee
Cuba Libre
Daiquiri
Funky Monkey
Harvey Funk
  (Charlie Wallbanger)
Hot Buttered Rum
Jamaican Coffee
  (Caribbean Coffee)
Long Island Iced Tea
Mai Tai
Paint Thinner
Piña Colada
Planter's Punch
Strawberry Daiquiri
Sunrise Colada
Zombie

SCHNAPPS (APPLE)

Jolly Rancher
Shiny Navel

SCHNAPPS (PEACH)

Fuzzy Navel
Jolly Rancher
Peaches and Cream
Woo Woo

SCHNAPPS (PEPPERMINT)

Candy Apple
Girl Scout Cookie
Moscow Moose
Peppermint Patty
Pepto Bismol
Snow Shoe

SCOTCH

Dry Rob Roy
Godfather
Harper House
Perfect Roy Roy
Rob Roy
Rusty Nail

SLOE GIN

Alabama Slammer
Jelly Bean
Sloe Comfortable Screw
Sloe Comfortable Screw
  Up Against the Wall
Sloe Gin Fizz
Sloe Screw (Cobra)
Sunset

SOUTHERN COMFORT

Alabama Slammer
Scarlet O'Hara
Sicilian Kiss
Sicilian Kiss Cocktail
Sloe Comfortable Screw
Sloe Comfortable Screw
  Up Against the Wall

INDEX

VODKA (cont.)

Topaz
Transfusion
Velvet Glove
Vodka Gibson
Vodka Gimlet
White Lightning
White Russian
Windjammer
Woo Woo
Yellow Canary

WHITE CREME DE CACAO

Angel's Wing
Pousse Cafe

WHITE CREME DE MENTHE

Patty Mint
Pousse Cafe
Runny Nose
Stinger

WILD TURKEY

Runny Nose
Snow Shoe

WINE

Kir (Chablis)
Spritzer
Wine Cooler

YUKON JACK

Snakebite